CW01095700

Building
Your
Business

THOROGOOD

THE PUBLISHING
BUSINESS OF THE
HAWKSMERE GROUP

Published by Thorogood Limited
12-18 Grosvenor Gardens
London SW1W 0DH.

Thorogood Limited is part of the
Hawksmere Group of Companies.

A CIP catalogue record for this Pocketbook is available
from the British Library.

ISBN 1 85418 079 7

Printed in Great Britain by Ashford Colour Press.

Designed and typeset by Paul Wallis at Thorogood.

Front cover: © Bridgeman Art Library
– *Apparition of the Chimney* by Giorgio de Chirico.

Business Action Pocketbooks

Business Action Pocketbooks are concise but comprehensive reference books designed to fit in your pocket or briefcase to be a ready source of business information. Each *Pocketbook* gives an introductory overview of a single topic and is followed by around 20 sections describing a particular aspect of that topic in more detail.

Pocketbooks will be of use to anyone involved in business. For owner managers and for managers in bigger businesses they will provide an introduction to the topic; for people already familiar with the topic they provide a ready reminder of key requirements. Each section concludes with a checklist of useful tips.

This book is based on *Business Information Factsheets* researched and written by enterprise and economic development agency, Project North East. Section contributors include Linda Jameson, Andrew Maville and Bill Waugh all of whom work at PNE. The series has been edited by David Irwin.

The information is checked by an independent expert to ensure, as far as possible, that it is accurate and up to date. However, neither the publishers nor the authors can accept any responsibility for any actions that you should take based on its contents. If you are in doubt about a proposed course of action, you should seek further professional advice.

Other titles in the 'Pocketbook' series

Business Action Pocketbooks are a series of concise but comprehensive reference books. Each one contains sections describing particular aspects of a topic in detail and checklists with useful tips.

Sales and Marketing

This *Pocketbook* is an excellent reference tool focusing on the overall process of sales and marketing. It will help give you a direction and a set of goals along with practical tips and techniques for successful market research, segmentation and planning, promoting, selling and exporting. It will help you take those first important steps towards establishing a presence in your market.

Managing and Employing People

Discover the key to successful people management by motivating, stimulating and rewarding your staff. Practical information and advice

Contents

Introduction

about recruiting staff, employee rights and obligations, effectively managing people and the legal aspects of employment are all covered in this *Pocketbook*.

Finance and Profitability

Practical tips and techniques for profitable management, including costing and budgeting, record keeping and using financial statements and understanding and finding investment are given in this *Pocketbook*. There is also advice on financial forecasting, monitoring performance against your plans and retaining effective financial control. This book will help ensure that your business is successful and profitable.

Developing Yourself and Your Staff

Team building, personal development, managing meetings, stimulating staff and quality management are all covered in a clear and practical way for the busy manager in this *Pocketbook*. By developing your people through teamwork, training and empowerment you are developing your business – this book tells you how.

Introduction

Growing your business

Strategic thinking

The overall concept of strategy is very simple. You have a goal and you do what is necessary to achieve that goal, though achieving a successful outcome may require some effort. There are, of course, enormous pressures on business both from within and outside the organisation. Bob Garratt, commenting on the Institute of Directors' publication, Standards for the Board, describes what he calls four directoral dilemmas. These dilemmas apply to anyone who is running a business:

- The proprietor must endeavour to be entrepreneurial and to drive the business forward whilst at the same time retaining effective control

- The proprietor must be sufficiently know-ledgeable about all the activities of the business to be answerable for its actions (even when small, but increasingly difficult as the business grows), yet must be able to stand back from day to day activities in order to take a longer term view of where the business is going and how to get there

- The proprietor must be aware of short term and local issues whilst also keeping up to date with the trends in the competitive market place and in the wider environment; and

- The proprietor needs to focus on the commercial needs of the business whilst acting responsibly and fairly to staff, business pressures and, particularly as the business grows, to the wider community.

Ideally all of these will be addressed during your strategic thinking.

It seems that a great number of books about strategy, or some element of it, are written every year. Some of them have a simple message, though in practice it is not always easy to see how to apply that message in a smaller business. Others are more complex, and the message itself is less clear, let alone how to apply it.

The message is simple: strategy gets you 'from here to there'. If you take control of the strategy, you can achieve great goals. The strategy itself can be simple – indeed, the simpler the strategy, the easier it will be to implement. What, then, are the characteristics of a successful strategy?

I believe they are these:

* First, businesses need a purpose – they must be clear about what they do

* Second, businesses need to know where they want to go – they must have vision – and ambition – perhaps demonstrated by using what American academics, John Collins and Gerry Porras refer to as 'big hairy audacious goals' and

* Thirdly, they need at least some idea of where the rest of the world is going – that is, foresight.

To maximise your chances of success in business, you need a purpose, you need goals, you need a plan, you need to monitor your performance against the plan and you may need occasionally to take corrective action to stay on course. A clear and simple direction will make leading the business far easier. To be effective you need regularly to look at your business's strengths and weaknesses and at the opportunities and threats posed by the environment in which you operate.

Strategy defines what you do to get you from where you are now to where you want to be, say, in three or five years' time. Peter Drucker asserts that strategy is what converts plans into results. Businesses set a purpose and define goals. The strategy must support the purpose. It must fit the environment in which the business works. It will be constrained by resource availability. It must be action focused. In Drucker's words, strategy 'converts what you want to do into accomplishment'.

Many small businesses think of strategic or long term planning as something that is only undertaken by large businesses. Henry Mintzberg argues that strategic planning is a contradiction in terms, in that it is not possible to plan and to be strategic simultaneously. Strategy may be about the future, but strategic actions take place in the present. Those actions do, of course, need to be consistent with longer term strategic thinking. Strategic thinking is simply a way of thinking about how to position your business *vis à vis* your customers and your competitors. Many businesses do have a clear idea of where they are heading and how they expect to get there; many more appear simply to be 'in business' without really having any clear vision. Stop for a moment… can you imagine the future? Of course you can – you have hopes and aspirations and you may already have goals and targets. So you have what Gary Hamal and CK Prahalad call 'strategic intent' – a desire to shape your future and an idea of what that future might look like. They go on to suggest that a strategic intent provides a framework of three elements: a sense of direction, a sense of discovery and a sense of destiny.

The businesses that survive and prosper are those that meet their customers' needs by providing benefits to them at prices which cover the cost of providing them and provide both sufficient profit for reinvestment and a share of the profit or a dividend large enough to satisfy the owners or the shareholders. To do this effectively, it is important to think strategically but it is also important to plan if the strategy is to be implemented effectively. Do you know how you intend to achieve your aspirations? If so, you have a strategy. It doesn't have to be complicated; indeed, the simpler you keep it, the easier it is to remember. Taking a strategic view of your business will help you to think about your over-arching goals and how you expect to achieve them. Having a strategy should not be seen as a straight jacket – but as a framework enabling you both to keep the business on course but also to exploit appropriate opportunities as they arise. The Japanese call this *hoshin kanri* – direction management. The strategy must be flexible, but without some long term objectives you will not be able to manage your direction.

Peter Drucker argues that businesses need to focus on the external environment in order to create a customer. Similarly, Michael Porter argues that the way a business positions itself in the market place is of paramount importance.

Johnson and Scholes note that effective strategies:

- Match the business's activities to the environment

- Match the business's activities to its available resources or its ability to attract extra resources

- Reflect the values and expectations of the business's stakeholders, particularly, their owners; and

- Impact on a business's long term direction.

More specifically, your task is to match effectively the business's competences (that is, its knowledge, expertise and experience) and resources with the opportunities and threats created by the market place.

Thinking strategically is important for every business, but it is particularly important for the smaller business, since smaller businesses may be more vulnerable than larger businesses to changes in the market place.

If you are reading this book, the chances are that you want to develop strategies which will help you to grow. As you grow, however, you may need to adjust your strategy. It may be worth mentioning, therefore, the likely stages of growth in your business and the ways in which businesses grow.

Stages of growth

An American academic, Larry Greiner suggests that businesses grow – or fail – through combinations of evolution and revolution – progressing through stages of creativity, direction, delegation, co-ordination and collaboration. A revolution at the end of each stage often precedes progress to the next stage.

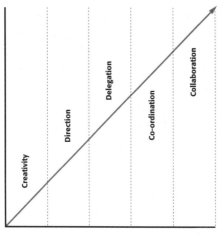

Source: Larry Greiner

7

In the creativity stage, the emphasis is on creating the product or service and creating a market for that product. The founders are usually entrepreneurially or technically oriented. Most businesses inevitably lack management and commercial experience at this stage; indeed, this is even worse where a business is started by a scientist or technologist whose motivation may stem from solving an interesting technical problem rather than from a desire to found a viable business. The structure is informal or non-existent. Communication is frequent and informal. This doesn't matter because the business is still pretty small. Control is exercised, if at all, simply through market results.

Twenty years ago it was highly unlikely that businesses would have started up other than on a local basis. Yet now, with the speed of technological innovation so great, some businesses, particularly technology based businesses will probably have started trading internationally almost from their first day – and some may even have been started with an international base. Whilst this may be very exciting it substantially increases the management control problems!

As the business grows, it experiences problems. Improving manufacturing efficiency may require greater knowledge. As the number of staff grows, it becomes more difficult to manage through informal communication. Procedures are needed for effective financial control. All this implies a need for a strong business manager, who provides direction.

Direction focuses on efficiency, a functional organisational structure, an accounting system with incentives, budgets and work standards, a more formal and impersonal system of communication and control through standards and cost centres.

However, the hierarchy becomes restrictive and there is a conflict between following procedures and taking initiatives. This implies a need for delegation.

Delegation emphasises market expansion. It gives staff greater responsibility and motivates them through profit centres and bonuses. Control is through reports and profit centre responsibility.

This, however, leads to a sense of loss of control and lack of co-ordination. Some businesses may react against this to the extent of taking back responsibilities.

If the firm progresses to the next stage, however, there is more emphasis on consolidation and systems for co-ordination with formal planning procedures, centralised control and review with control imposed through plans and investment centres.

This can lead to too much bureaucracy and the procedures taking precedence over problem solving. This leads to a need for collaboration.

Collaboration implies a participative management style with a focus on problem solving through teamwork and, commonly, a matrix type management structure. There is less emphasis on rigid procedures and more emphasis on management development and mutual goal setting.

Any of you who have grown a business to the stage where it employs a number of people engaged in a range of activities will probably have experienced these stages.

I mention these stages of growth because the points at which a business recognises a need to move on – changing management structures, changing control systems, etc – often coincide with a need for a rethink about strategy and, sometimes, a need for more investment. Furthermore external financiers will have matching requirements – strong management, effective control systems, etc. And businesses which understand where they are on the growth curve will be in a better position to argue their case with prospective funders.

Values, style and behaviour

Working is not just a way to earn a living, but also an opportunity to create an environment for people who share similar values to work together. Personal values affect the way that we behave, the way that an organisation behaves depends on its staff's beliefs and behaviours. The most successful organisations are those both where the staff share similar values and moral principles since these guide individual and corporate behaviour, and also where those values reinforce the organisation's purpose.

Collins and Porras argue that, when properly harnessed, shared values create 'a sense of purpose beyond making money that guides and inspires people throughout the organisation'. Many organisations do have some sort of culture and philosophy but, too often, it remains implicit. Increasingly, however, private sector companies are becoming more explicit about their corporate values, often attempting to encapsulate them into a statement of beliefs. An organisation's values should provide an essential and enduring set of general guiding principles. They are something to strive for in spite of changes to the environment. Values might include the need to achieve, the desire to help others, the belief that an organisation must behave ethically, the desire to develop one's own abilities and expertise, etc.

The behaviour of an organisation will be embodied in the organisation's management style and will be manifested in the way it relates to staff and in the way it relates to clients. In turn, stakeholders' perceptions of the business will depend on how they see the business behave. Do they see a helpful organisation? A caring organisation? A ruthless organisation?

Some people have difficulty in separating their personal values with those that they perceive that their employer finds desirable. You may prefer, therefore, to prepare a company 'philosophy' which encapsulates both of these.

Christopher Bartlett and Sumantra Ghoshal believe that being clear about your beliefs and values probably helps businesses to 'attract and retain employees who identify with their values and become deeply committed to the organisation that embodies them'. They go on to suggest that individuals 'extract the most basic sense of purpose from the personal fulfilment they derive from being part of any organisation'. It is, therefore, essential that you, as you employ staff, rise to that challenge by creating 'an energising corporate purpose'.

Purpose

A statement of purpose or a mission statement, guides the activities of a business. It is what 'you do'. Defining a purpose is a pre-requisite for effective planning. Ideally, it should be easily understood by all the stakeholders, that is, the owners, the customers, the staff and anyone else with a stake in the business. The purpose statement should be the over-riding factor in guiding an organisation. Ideally, it should not only define the business it is in but also differentiate it from its competitors.

Peter Drucker argues that the purpose of business must be to create a customer. What the customer buys and considers to be of value determines what a business is, what it produces and whether it will prosper. In other words, businesses should be market driven. Drucker goes on to argue, therefore, that the two basic functions of any business are marketing and innovation. Businesses which are market driven respond to the needs of their customers. Businesses which are product driven start with a product and then try to persuade customers to buy it. Customers buy benefits – if the features of the product or service do not confer the benefits sought by customers, then customers will not buy. It is perhaps worth noting, however, that customers cannot always articulate the benefits they would like – as Sony demonstrated with their Walkman.

Some businesses have very long mission statements which set out all the organisation's objectives. A short mission, however, is more likely to excite and inspire the stakeholders and is more likely to be remembered by the staff. Blooming Marvellous, for example, defines its purpose thus: 'We design, make and market clothes for the fashion conscious mother to be.' This statement defines precisely the activities undertaken by the company and their target customers. Apple Computer, in a similar vein, say 'our goal has always been to create the world's friendliest, most understandable computers – computers that empower the individual.'

Arguably, visionary companies have a core ideology which encompasses core values and a sense of purpose. Collins and Porras suggest that core ideology provides 'a set of basic precepts that plant a fixed stake in the ground. This is who we are; this is what we stand for; this is what we're all about.' However you define it, the important thing to remember is that the core ideology should guide and inspire everyone inside the business.

Vision

Purpose expresses what the business does, but it is vision which drives the business forward. It is vision which sets a direction for the business. Vision is about having challenging, but achievable, goals with defined time scales. In particular, you may find it helps to set what Collins and Porras call 'big hairy audacious goals'. You may choose to pull these goals together into a single vision: a statement of your desired position within your best guess of the future environment. This requires you to think about the environment in which you are currently operating and the likely environment in the future. Keep to a reasonable timescale, say up to five years.

Do not make the process too complicated. You do need to have some idea of the environment in which you will operate, although most small organisations are more likely to have to react to the environment rather than being able to influence it. Similarly, the consequences of getting it wrong will be different for a small organisation compared, say, to Shell's decision whether to invest billions of pounds on a new North Sea gas platform. If an organisation's vision reflects its shared values then this will reinforce the likelihood of achieving the vision.

Once you have defined your vision, then you can think about what you have to do to achieve it. This involves setting strategic and operational objectives.

The importance of thinking ahead

There are many external pressures on any organisation. These include competitors' activities.

This probably sounds daunting, but it is easy to break down the planning process into a number of levels. Henry Mintzberg argues that *planning is about preparing for the inevitable, pre-empting the undesirable and controlling the controllable*. Without at least some planning to determine how you will achieve your goals, there will be nothing to control.

There is no magic formula for success. Management writers and academics like to coin new terms like total quality management or Kaizen or business process re-engineering. But simply introducing one or more of these ideas does little to help the business. What does help the business is having a clear idea of what your customers or potential customers want; a clear idea of how you can deliver your product or service to them at a cost lower than the price they are prepared to pay; and, a clear idea of how to stay ahead of your competitors.

Planning can help with:

- *Focusing ideas* – the process of planning forces boards and staff to think through and refine their organisations' goals and objectives

- *Assessing viability* – regularly ensuring that there will be sufficient income to cover all the costs and make a profit

- *Maintaining control* – the most effective weapon for control is knowledge – knowing where the business is now, how it is performing and where it is going

- *Developing foresight* – planning as a continuous activity encourages the identification of opportunities; a plan can then be formulated to take advantage of these. In addition, planning helps in the identification of threats, so that these can be avoided or mitigated.

Defining a purpose and agreeing goals which reflect your values and beliefs will provide you with the framework that you need. Creating a strategy will put in place the long term guidance to enable the business to move towards achievement of its goals and consequent success.

Redefining those long term objectives as short term operational targets will provide suitable milestones. Measuring performance will enable you to see how well the business is doing and, if necessary, take corrective action.

Do not forget to watch the market place and the wider environment. Changes may affect your policy and will almost certainly affect your strategic objectives.

As you start to achieve your goals, set new ones. Even in a small company a three or five year strategy will probably be in need of renewal half way through the time period. Failure to redefine goals regularly probably indicates that effective review of performance, resources, resource availability and the environment is not being undertaken and the business is drifting rather than being driven along. Aim to maximise use of your resources, but do not over extend yourself.

Policy sets a long term view and reflects how the organisation sees itself within the external environment. Strategic thinking is similarly long term, but is more about the internal operation of the organisation; operations are clearly internal and tend to be short term. The way that the organisation operates will affect the way it is perceived by outsiders and the way in which the business may find itself accountable if it 'misbehaves'.

Remember that the ideal strategy is simple, clear and measurable – and will help you to ensure that you achieve your stake in the future.

Policy   **Strategy**

Review   **Implementation**

Growth,
strategy
and business
planning

part
one

Growth,
strategy
and business
planning

part
one

1 **Could you run your own business?**

This section looks at how to assess your ability to run your own business.

Introduction

Establishing your own business is a very rewarding experience, but there are also great risks and pressures associated with it. It is not enough just to have a good, viable idea. You also need to have the right skills and the appropriate temperament to make the opportunity succeed. You will have to win the confidence of the bank, customers and your employees. It is important to look honestly at your own capabilities before you decide to proceed with your business idea.

Assessing the risks

Starting your own business is by definition an uncertain thing. Using the evidence of your market research you can systematically assess the chances of your business succeeding. An important part of that assessment is your ability to implement the strategies, and carry out the tasks that will make the business work. This is hard because:

- It is difficult to arrive at an objective opinion of your own abilities – you may underestimate or overestimate yourself

- It is hard to know exactly how you will react in circumstances which you have never previously encountered

- You never know how you may develop in the long term – you may be surprised at what you can do when you have to.

In the end, there are no final answers to such questions. It is important to find out as much as you can about what sort of person you are. You must be honest and objective. Discuss the project with friends, colleagues and relations. Whenever possible look for hard evidence to back up your analysis. What have you done that proves you have this or that ability?

Motives

Whatever your abilities, if the motivation is strong enough, you will have more chance of overcoming the problems. Examine your motives closely. If they are genuine, they will help you. On the other hand, you may find that fundamentally you are starting for the wrong reasons. Surveys reveal a number of common reasons for starting a business:

Independence

This is perhaps the most common reason given for starting a business. Working for someone else can be irksome, but you still need to be disciplined and able to get on with others when you work for yourself.

Job satisfaction

People often want to do the job in their own way, and this leads them into self-employment. A deep interest in the activity, and real ideas about how you could innovate, are a real asset.

Achievement and success

There is certainly a lot of glory attached to running your own business, but make sure that you are not trying to prove that you are something you are not. The venture may even fail – can you deal with this?

Money

This is not usually enough in itself. Wealth is by no means guaranteed. In particular, beware of starting a business when you have no other choice. A positive vision is important.

Pressures

The pressures of being self-employed are inescapable. You will be staking practically everything on your own ability. If it goes wrong, there will be no-one to blame but yourself. You may have to work long hours, and there will be times when things get on top of you. You may well get into debt in order to finance the enterprise. You will need to maintain your faith in your business, often in the face of heavy criticism. It's tough at the top. If you employ people, you need to be positive and show leadership all the time, even when you do not feel like it. There will be times when you need to be tough and prepared to discipline difficult employees. There will be times when you feel lonely and isolated. You need to be polite and helpful even when an awkward customer is giving you a hard time.

This may sound like a nightmare, but you need to be the sort of person who relishes such challenges. Some of the best entrepreneurs are those who thrive on pressure. To cope, you need a lot of confidence in yourself, and the energy and toughness to get through the bad times.

Age and experience

There is no doubt that it helps to have at least some experience. Surveys reveal that many successful businesses have been started by people in their thirties who have some management experience. On the other hand, young people have some particular advantages. They have fewer domestic commitments, plenty of energy, new ideas and the potential to develop and adapt to the challenges of self-employment. Those who typically succeed in the Livewire scheme are in their mid twenties with some education and experience behind them, but still at an early stage in their careers. Having said all this, there is no ideal age for starting a business (for further details on Livewire refer to page 220).

Skills and qualifications

Technical skills

Qualifications relevant to the business activity are obviously important. You need to be able to achieve professional standards of work in order to compete in the marketplace. Customers and lending institutions may require that you have the right qualifications. Certain businesses require exceptional ability, eg design skills, artistic skill, technical skill. What evidence can you offer to prove your ability, eg have you won awards for your work?

Business skills

Business skills are essential. It is important to understand the principles of business and management including marketing, strategic planning, accounts, personnel management, etc. You can get basic training in management skills. A relevant diploma or degree would also be an asset.

Leadership skills

If you are happy for the operation to remain small in the long run, then you can continue to concentrate upon the processes, etc without worrying about personnel management issues. If however you expect the business to grow, inevitably you will have to employ people, and the ability to show leadership and to manage people will be critical. Many people turn to self-employment in order to have the freedom to work independently. Sometimes this is because they have difficulty working with others. In the long term, if the business is to grow, the proprietor must learn this skill. Many promising enterprises fail to grow because their owners fail to make this transition. Are you good with people? Do you have management experience? Did you enjoy working in a managerial role?

Selling skills

All businesses require an element of selling. Initially it is important to persuade people to support you, and crucial to be able to win over potential customers. It is possible to learn basic selling techniques, but being outgoing and articulate are equally important.

Organisational skills

To generate sufficient income, small businesses must be well organised and efficient. It is important to be the sort of person who can organise, plan ahead, manage their time and have the discipline to set and meet deadlines.

Personality

The characteristics suitable for successful self-employment depend very much upon the type of activity involved. A complicated technical operation requires intelligent, well qualified and organised people. A straightforward business idea (eg one person and a delivery van) does not require any special skills. Some businesses suit brash self-confident types but many are successfully run by people who are quiet and shy.

There is no single type of self-employed person, but experience has shown that there are some things which successful self-employed people often have in common:

- Logical, perceptive, organised, responsible – good at getting things done

- Extrovert, confident

- Good communicators, able to get their point across

- Sociable, good leader

- Single-minded – but able to take advice

- Flexible, adaptable

- Opportunist, risk taker, ambitious

- Hard working, committed, determined, 'get up and go' type

- Tough – often the best test of a successful person is their ability to handle failure!

- Individual – not afraid to stand out from the crowd

- Creative, imaginative – always coming up with new ideas.

This list is not definitive, but it should give you an idea of the challenges ahead. You do not need to have all these characteristics. You will develop and grow with the experience. If you intend to start up as a partnership, look for complementary characteristics. The best partnerships are ones where the partners have different abilities and strengths to contribute to the business.

Family commitments

Many of those who successfully start their own business have the backing of their family – even if this is only in the form of moral support. You will be under pressure, working long hours. Your family must be prepared for the impact this can have on family life. Ideally, it helps if you can get some finance from a friendly family source. At the other extreme, ensure that your long term family commitments can accommodate the risks that self-employment can bring, especially in terms of income.

USEFUL TIPS

- *Give yourself experiences that test out your abilities eg travel by yourself abroad, undertake a difficult project.*

- *The process of assessing your ideas never really ends. Sometimes it is necessary to go right to the brink of starting the business before you realise it is not for you. If the time is not right now (eg you need more experience, more money, etc) it may still be an option for the future.*

- *Get advice about your business idea, and your own capabilities, from an experienced business adviser.*

2 Writing a business plan

This section gives suggestions about the contents and layout of a business plan.

Introduction

A business plan is a complete description of a business and its plans for the next 1-5 years. It explains what the business does (or will do); outlines who will buy the product or services and why; includes financial forecasts; and indicates how much money (if any) is needed.

Use

Most people only write a business plan when they need to raise finance for their business. However, the ideal business plan can be thought of like a road map – you define your destination (in other words, your strategic objectives) and the business plan then acts as your route plan for getting there. You should, therefore, revise your business plan each year, set targets and prepare financial forecasts. You should do this regardless of whether you need to raise extra money.

Contents of a business plan

Below is a list of all the items a business plan could contain. Not all of them will be appropriate in every case, so do not worry if it seems best to miss out a section. The cover page should give the business name and the names and addresses of the proprietors.

Summary

The summary should briefly describe the business and highlight the key objectives. You should probably write this last.

The business

a)   Describe it and its history to date

b)   How does its performance compare with its competitors?

c)   Give copies of records if already started – profit and loss account, balance sheet, bank records, present funding

d)   Major accomplishments.

Product or service

a)   Describe it in layman's terms!

b)   What are the advantages of your product or service; what need does it fill; what are its unique features?

c) Give details of patent or copyright or statutory requirements if appropriate

d) Discuss competitive products.

The market

a) Give estimated demand in the short and long term and explain why this demand is expected

b) Who are the target customers?

c) Who are competitors and possible future competitors? Comparison of product /service; why is yours distinctive? Advantages of your business over competitors

d) Give an appraisal of the competition.

Marketing plan

a) Give details of target markets, and show that a market exists; make an estimate of your current and predicted market share

b) Explain the pricing policy

c) Explain how the product or service will be promoted

d) Give details of the selling and distribution methods

e) Explain the longer term plans of the business

f) Give details of orders or interest by potential customers.

Operations

a) Highlight any competitive advantages

b) State where the business is (or will be) located

c) Describe the premises and the equipment the business has, or will need

d) Describe the production process

e) Personnel requirements.

Management and organisation

a) What are the strengths of the people involved?

b) If there are apparent weaknesses explain how they will be overcome

c) Give brief CV details including age, education, experience, etc of all key personnel.

Financial information

a) Give start up or expansion and budget information; include historical statements if already trading

b) Costing and pricing

c) Give financial forecasts including cashflow, profit and loss and balance sheet projections, omitting any grant or loan which may be required. Give the break even point (ie the level of sales at which the business will start to make a profit)

d) Include details of personal savings to be invested

e) Give details of all personal financial commitments (personal survival budget)

f) Explain all your assumptions.

Financial requirements

a) Give details of how much is needed, when and from whom

b) What overdraft facility will be required?

c) Specify any other grants or loans, such as Regional Enterprise grants or Local Authority grants, which have been obtained or applied for.

Security

Give details of any assets available as security.

● *Content*

Most bankers and other funders like to see concise 8-10 page business plans with extra information as appendices. If there is too much, it is less likely to be read carefully; if too little, you will be asked for more details. The more money you are looking for the more comprehensive you need to be.

● *Getting the information and drafting the plan*

Your business plan will change almost daily as you collect information. If you have and can use a computer, you will find this very useful; otherwise, it is best to write the plan after you have done all your preparatory work. It is always useful to try out the plan on a counsellor at your nearest local enterprise agency (or enterprise trust in Scotland).

● *Presentation*

Good presentation can make a big difference to portraying a professional image and, therefore, to raising the funds you need. Add a cover page giving the name of your business, your name and address. If possible, have your plan professionally bound.

● **Funding**

Don't underestimate your funding requirements. Make sure you take into account the development of your business over 2-3 years.

● **Verification**

Make sure you refer to any external publications or data to support your information. This will show you have taken time to prepare and will appear much more professional.

● **Appendices**

The CVs of key personnel, plus any other details required, (such as technical descriptions, market statistics or financial figures) should be included as appendices to keep the body of the business plan short and uncluttered.

● **Above all:**

> **Be honest**
>
> **Be logical**
>
> **Be consistent**
>
> **Be realistic.**

3 Mission, vision and strategic objectives

Businesses which have a clear idea of their purpose, where they are going and how they are going to get there will dramatically increase their chances of succeeding. This section suggests some ways of thinking through these issues.

Culture and values

Running a business is not just a way to earn a living, but also an opportunity for people to work, live and relate together. The most successful businesses are those where the staff share similar values. Many businesses attempt to encapsulate these shared values into a values statement which sets out their beliefs. A business's values are likely to affect its culture or, if you like, 'the way we do things round here'.

Octo Industrial Design, for example, states its culture thus: 'At Octo we have stacks of energy and boundless enthusiasm. We are an active and dedicated team who care, support each other and have fun'. This says a lot about the staff, but it also points towards how they expect to help their clients.

Values and behaviour are closely linked. If staff share the values of the business, they will be reflected in individual and corporate behaviour. Many large businesses develop value statements which talk about how they relate to customers. This is fine, but belief in these values must really be shared by staff if the desired effect on behaviour is to be achieved. This relationship between values and behaviour is particularly important when businesses want to change their culture. For example, many businesses are currently encouraging their staff to think about quality and to build into their culture behaviour which reinforces the quality of their product or service.

The proprietor's style of management will also have a major impact on the culture of the business.

Mission

It is fashionable these days to have a 'mission statement'. At its simplest, a mission is a statement of purpose which guides the activities of your business. It is what 'you do'. Ideally it should be simply understood by staff, customers, financial backers, etc. For example, Blooming Marvellous describes its mission as 'We design, make and market clothes for the fashion conscious mother to be'. As can be seen from this statement, they have carefully defined what they do, their specific product and their market niche. Octo Industrial Design has defined its mission thus: 'Octo's purpose is to produce consistently successful design solutions for clients who aspire to high quality design'.

Service businesses often find it easy to seek and take on work outside their main activities without thinking about whether they should. If all opportunities are measured against a carefully worded mission, you will be less likely to be diverted into activities which 'take your eye off the ball'. Once you have defined your purpose, you should not normally need to reconsider it. Spend time thinking about what you do. Consider your strengths and weaknesses. Ask yourself 'what business am I in?' Parker Pen, for example, sees itself in the gift business and positions itself as competing against Ronson lighters. Metro Radio sees itself, not in the radio business, but in the 'commodity business' – selling advertising opportunities.

Vision

Defining purpose expresses what the business does. But it is 'vision' which drives the business forward. Vision is about having challenging, but achievable, goals with defined time scales. It is simply a statement of your desired competitive position within your best guess of the future environment.

Start by considering the opportunities for and threats to your business. Think about what the working environment is going to be like in, say, five years time. Summarise your objectives into a single statement. For example: 'Octo aims to be respected as a leading design group working throughout Europe'. This business has chosen not to disclose publicly the timescale to which it is working, but it has set one by which it hopes to achieve their vision.

If you have a realistic vision, eventually you will achieve it. This is good for morale for you and your staff. When you think you are approaching achievement of your vision, start again with a new vision.

Strategic objectives

Once you have set your long-term aim (in other words, vision) you are able to consider what needs to be done to achieve it. These strategic objectives will probably cover marketing, finance, staff development, etc. They may also include quality, diversification, acquisitions, etc.

Try to be succinct. Set milestones. You can use absolute targets, or targets relative to previous years or targets relative to your competitors (which will allow for external factors). For example:

- 'We will increase sales by £100,000 pa'

- 'We will increase sales by 25%'

- 'We will increase our market share by 2% pa'.

Strategic objectives should be kept relatively short, but should be clear. As with the vision they need to be challenging but achievable.

For everyday purposes, the strategic objectives may need to be split down into a series of operational objectives which will also have performance measures, targets and timescales. These can then be used to monitor progress and control the business.

Just a tool

Remember that all these concepts are simply tools for your business. Use them as you think fit. Some businesses use some or all of their values, mission and vision in their marketing, for example. Many use them to help think about future direction. Do not get carried away with them. Many businesses are successful without ever giving any of these concepts a thought – but having a clear idea of your future, setting clear targets and achieving those targets will help you to be more successful.

USEFUL TIPS

- *It can be very difficult to think through values, mission and vision. Do not be afraid to ask for help. Often your local enterprise agency will be able to provide appropriate facilitation support.*

- *If you already employ staff, everyone needs to be involved in business strategy.*

- *This is inevitably a very short description of some complex tools. Read widely about the subject.*

4 Introducing a strategic review process

This section looks at how to institute a process to review and update your business strategy. Strategic ideas and terms are discussed in other sections.

Introduction

Most people running a small business have some sort of long-term vision of where they are taking their business. Many are also well aware of the value of producing a written business plan. Too often, however, the strategy document is neglected and gets out of date once the business has started. *Strategic planning should be seen as an essential function of the business like personnel management or accounting for example*. It is important to recognise that unless time and resources are allocated to the process of producing a plan, and doing the necessary background research, strategic planning will continue to be done on an ad hoc basis. In an ever changing, increasingly competitive environment, only businesses with positive ideas about how to deal with the threats and opportunities of the future will survive and prosper.

What is strategic review?

Strategic review is a systematic approach which aims to ensure that strategic planning takes place regularly, that it is carried out in a systematic manner and that all relevant views and information are taken into account. This section looks at the setting up of a review process, rather than the subject of strategic analysis itself. All the same, any process that you set up should reflect the process of analysis, ie gathering and assimilating information, considering a range of options and identifying the best one(s) for the business. At all times the options are evaluated in terms of the business's objectives. The review process will normally follow an annual schedule and will include a review of existing strategy, the competitive environment, business operations, consultation, agreement and production of a revised plan. It is crucial to act upon plans and to assess the results before making further plans. This should lead to a 'loop' of continuous improvement whereby planning becomes more and more acute in the light of experience. Scenario planning is increasingly used to help businesses prepare contingencies for dramatic change in the future. You look at what the business would need to do if certain key influences on the business changed, eg a dramatic price rise in a key material cost. A number of different scenarios are usually developed.

Why have a strategy?

The pace of change

The pace of change is increasing and set to increase further. New technology is changing the way people live and work. New products and services are in demand and businesses need to react more and more quickly. The Single Market has created new threats and opportunities. The World Trade Organisation (WTO) will lead to further international competition. Economic development in Eastern Europe and the Pacific Rim will increasingly impinge upon the traditional economic powers. All businesses must find ways to ensure that they are aware of the changes that affect them and take active measures to address them.

Improving strategic decisions

It is widely accepted that creating time to plan leads to more effective solutions. A systematic planning process will improve business performance by generating imaginative solutions and identifying economies and efficiencies. Decisions will be more effective if based upon accurate information. Strategic planning should ensure that all available factors, knowledge and ideas are considered before decisions are taken.

Measuring performance and involving staff
Assessing past performance is just as important as making plans for the future. This is particularly important in terms of management. A strategic approach will help you to assess how well individuals and departments have done in relation to the targets set. This will be particularly important if you wish to introduce performance related pay. Long-term planning is an excellent opportunity to involve and consult with employees. Planning together can enhance team spirit. The resulting targets should be more credible and achievable.

Setting up a review process

Responsibility
Someone must be responsible for ensuring that the review takes place in the correct manner, at the appropriate time. In the small business, this is an obvious role for the person in overall charge. In larger businesses, co-ordination may be delegated, eg to the person in charge of marketing or market research.

Developing a process

The first step will be to decide how the process itself should be carried out. This process should be committed to paper. Everyone concerned should be aware of how it works. You may decide to file a copy of the review process in your handbook (if you have one). Strategy review is usually carried out on an annual schedule (looking at a time horizon of between three and five years) culminating in the agreement and circulation of the final strategy document. With experience you will be able to improve the process. Ask the people involved how they found the process and how it could be improved for the future.

A strategy document

A strategy document is of course the focus of the review process. It encapsulates the results of the review and provides individuals with a reminder of strategic objectives. It also forms the basis for starting the next review. A strategy document will be used for long-term plans, the business plan for the shorter term plans which progress the business towards achieving strategic objectives. Normally the document will be your current business plan.

Gathering information

Information gathering is a very important element of strategic review. Ideally someone should be responsible for gathering relevant information on a continual basis. Usually there will be no active research process going on. All the same, staff will come across relevant information all the time, eg a new competitor, a new product, new regulations affecting the industry, etc. These may be in the form of cuttings or samples, and should be filed for use at the appropriate time. On occasions research may be especially commissioned, or a member of staff may be commissioned to carry out an investigation. Another option is for each member of the planning team to undertake each element of the research and review process (eg external market, internal activities, etc). It is important that all relevant information is fed into the strategic planning process. At the same time, this must be done selectively to prevent overload. Staff should also be encouraged to submit ideas before formal meetings take place.

Consultation meetings

Meetings related to strategy development should be managed and structured systematically. They should be an active part of the process and will frequently last all day. Plan a programme and circulate it well in advance. Make sure you follow the programme and stay on schedule. Plan proceedings to follow the logical analysis process, eg discussing and digesting information, looking at a number of options, deciding on the best course of action. Some quite strong 'shaping' of proceedings may be necessary to progress things, eg pre-prepared presentations laying out a framework for discussion at each stage. Be imaginative. Sessions should to be varied and stimulating. Consider sessions which allow small groups to work together on particular issues and to report back to the main session. In addition, sub-groups may be commissioned to work on particular areas before the main review session. Make sure that proceedings are well facilitated. If you do not have the necessary skills, bring in someone who does.

It helps if you can arrange to hold at least one of your review meetings away from the business. 'Away days' can help staff to take a fresh look at things without interruption. Consider building recreation, team building and other training into sessions.

Consider the extent to which you include people. A small group (eg three or four) responsible for key areas will be easier to manage and more able to translate discussions into real actions. Wider employee involvement is always valuable but can be counter-productive if too many ideas have to be ignored. Departmental groups can meet, feeding their recommendations on to the executive group.

Implementation

When the strategy document has been finalised, it should be circulated as widely as possible. Consider circulating a summary in a distinctive readable form or as an insert for your business handbook. Clearly this does not necessarily guarantee implementation and specific targets will usually be negotiated with the staff concerned on a more direct basis. All the same, do not discard the document. Remind yourself of the contents on a frequent basis (eg once a month) and use it actively in your planning meetings. This will also have the effect of stimulating further thoughts for future reviews.

USEFUL TIPS

- *Develop a procedure to ensure that planning takes place. Schedule the stages of the planning process into your diary. Keep the process as simple as possible*

- *Strategic review is essentially consultative. Ultimately you will decide on the best* course of action. This makes things manageable, but it is important that people understand your decisions. Take on board all suggestions. Consider producing a document which records all views. Try to show why you have chosen one option rather than another

- Many businesses find it useful to carry out planning sessions away from the business. This should reduce the chance of interruption and help people to take a fresh look at the business

- Consider getting an independent consultant or business adviser to facilitate planning sessions. They can bring objectivity as well as expertise. There may be grants available towards the cost of this; enquire at your local Business Link or Department of Trade and Industry regional office

- Find out more about current strategic planning theory

- Market research assignments (eg postal questionnaires, etc) are ideal for students on placement, provided you select the right person and supervise them properly. Contact your local business studies colleges for details.

5 Understanding your competitors

This section looks at ways to assess your competitors.

Introduction

Before entering a market you have to decide if you will be able to compete with the established providers of goods and services. Once established you need to be aware of potential threats from new entrants to the market. Understanding your competitors and developing ways to distinguish yourself from them is a critical factor influencing the development of a business strategy. The need to be competitive is a basic fact of commercial life. Direct competition exists when rival businesses produce comparable products. Indirect competition exists when firms produce products that achieve the same end or benefits for the user. A business's potential profitability and survival depend on the behaviour of the competition.

Effects of competition

Lower prices

Competition forces firms to strive for efficiency. Firms limit their use of resources (ie raw materials, labour, etc) so that products/services can be produced at minimum cost. Prices for goods and services reflect production costs, so cost effectiveness results in lower costs to the consumer.

Higher quality products/services

Consumers are always trying to buy the highest quality product at the best price. Increased levels of competition encourage firms to produce high quality products with less variation in quality at a given price level.

Variety of goods and services

As firms actively seek to exploit untouched markets, new products and services are created, anticipating potential demand. Firms also respond to specialised demands. As a result, a large range of products and services are placed on the market.

The competitive environment

Competitive environments can be characterised as open, fierce or stable. Each is linked to the life-cycle of the product or industry under consideration.

Open

An open environment is an emerging or growing market where many companies are entering the market but no one firm dominates. Companies are not competing head-on, rather they are exploring the market's potential by marketing different products. Prices may be high, reflecting the weak competitive environment and low level of consumer product knowledge. Product value is generally untested.

Fierce

A fierce competitive environment is characterised by a mature market where many firms are vying for market share. Products are more alike. Both large and small companies enter and exit the market continuously, creating a volatile environment. The market may be dominated by a few companies. The high level of competition and consumer product knowledge improves the value and quality of the product while reducing prices.

Stable

A stable environment exists for a mature market in decline where the market is predictable. Established firms monopolise the market. New entrants pose little threat.

Understanding the competitive environment

The competitive environment which you are operating in may be characterised in terms of the various forces at work (Michael Porter, *A Competitive Strategy*, 1980). Each element assumes different levels of prominence depending on the industry.

Rivalry among existing firms

A rivalry develops when one or more firms feel the need or see a chance to improve their competitive position. Competitor moves are met by rival firms' countermoves. Profit margins are squeezed due to increased competition.

Threats from new entrants

New entrants to a market place new restrictions on existing competition. The seriousness of the threat depends on the barriers to market entry and the reaction of existing competition. Market entry barriers can include economies of scale, product differentiation, switching costs, gaining access to distribution channels and government policy.

Threats from substitute products

You also compete to an extent with businesses which produce substitute products. Substitute products are those products that meet the same customer requirements, eg airlines compete with buses, railway systems and cars. The availability of substitute products can limit profit potential.

Bargaining power of buyers

Powerful buyers can force prices down, and extract concessions in quality and services from firms in an industry by decreasing profits.

Bargaining power of suppliers

Powerful suppliers are able to increase prices and develop terms in their favour.

Developing a competitive strategy

A competitive strategy must be formulated in order to reach your profit potential. Three competitive strategies are outlined below.

Overall cost leadership strategy

This approach requires a programme to lower costs and increase efficiency. Prices are lowered and hopefully turnover is increased as a way to put pressure on competitors. Economies of scale are realised after developing experience in producing the product. A low cost position allows a business to continue to make profits after the competition competes their profits away. This position defends against powerful buyers, allows for greater flexibility in responding to input and cost increases by suppliers, discourages entrants because high initial costs are needed to achieve long-term cost advantages and develops a favourable position in relation to substitute products. This strategy works well with unsophisticated buyers. However, it develops a price ceiling which is difficult to penetrate later. Price cutting may cause rival firms to cut prices, resulting in a price war.

Differentiation

The differentiation strategy involves identifying customers needs and developing products / services to meet their needs. It focuses on offering products that are perceived industry wide as being unique. This strategy works well for undifferentiated products because a firm can differentiate a product from non-product features; eg service, selection, convenience, advertising/marketing, method of delivery, guarantee improvement and warranties, etc. Higher margins can result from this strategy allowing for flexibility when dealing with suppliers, and mitigating buyer power. Customer loyalty is created, thus discouraging new entrants.

Specialisation

Specialisation is focusing on a specific buyer group, segment of the product line, or geographic area with the aim to serve a narrowly defined market. The idea behind specialisation is that a firm serves a limited market more effectively and more efficiently than a firm that competes more broadly.

Know your competitors

Identify, profile and rank your individual competitors. This will help you understand and compare the information you gather. Here are some suggestions for analysing your competition.

- Overall number of direct competitors and number of indirect competitors.

- Competitor location, size, share of the market, sales structure, profit growth, research and development spending and commercial and industrial associations.

- Competitor strengths and weaknesses eg, in terms of location, size, related products, image, contacts, reputation, financial, speed of reaction to changes in the market etc.

- Competition and the four Ps.

  a) *Promotion*. The promotion techniques, media channels and advertising methods used by the competitor.

  b) *Price*. The competitor's pricing strategies, credit and discount practices /guarantees.

  c) *Place*. Channels of distribution, export agents, licence agreement, franchises etc, used by the competitor.

d) *Product*. The competitor's products and services, size and diversity of product range.

- Trends within the competitive environment include the number and type of companies entering and exiting the market, the length of competitor's time spent in the market, and the factors contributing to their entry and exit.

Benchmarking

Benchmarking is a new approach to assessing how competitive your business is by globally recognised standards of performance in measurable areas of business operations. Bob Camp, a world authority on the subject, has described it as 'the search for those best practices that will lead to the superior performance of a company'. Benchmarking is not just another label for comparing your business to others. It is a recognised process whereby the search for best practice in all processes is built into the business operation. Those involved need to fully understand how the process works, preferably through training. Top management must be fully committed. The process can involve profound organisational change and the implementation of the latest quality management methods.

Market intelligence

It is all too easy to forget about what the others are doing in your absorption with your own business activities. Ensure that you obtain regular supplies of information about other businesses, and that you set aside time to read it. Reading will range from browsing the business pages of your local newspaper, to purchasing the latest market report on your sector. Place a value on the information you need and build the cost into your budgets.

Information on your competitors can be found amongst the following sources; trade press, trade fairs, trade associations, customers, distributors, retailers, suppliers, books, government publications, market research companies, business advisers (accountants, bankers, etc.), Dun and Bradstreet, Mintel or Keynote market research reports, local press, quality press, market reports, annual reports, libraries, databases, periodicals and (never to be underestimated) *Yellow Pages*. You should visit your competitors to observe buyers, traffic, product range, promotional techniques and quality of service.

The information you compile should be evaluated and stored in a manageable form. If possible, write recent developments into your business plan as they happen.

- *Constantly monitor and keep up to date files on your competitors.*

- *Familiarise yourself with the competition policy within the European Union. This policy is comprised of merger control regulations and Article 85 and 86 of the Treaty of Rome. The Articles are designed to ensure that trade between member states takes place on the basis of free and fair competition, where firms do not create unfair trade barriers.*

- *With the advent of the single market, it is particularly important to monitor the activities of rival European companies.*

6 Leadership

This section looks at leadership in small firms.

Introduction

A leader is a person who gives other people direction and guidance. Some people lead by example, others by issuing commands. In business settings, a leader may be someone to whom others look because they hold a recognised position of authority (eg the owner/manager of a company or a foreman), or they can be individuals within the organisation who influence the actions of others through force of personality.

Leadership roles differ in many different situations. In the small business, leadership qualities are quite recognisable. A leader influences group behaviour in order to achieve goals. Good leadership is essential to business performance. However, there is no one best style of leadership – a leadership style that works for one person or in one situation might not necessarily work elsewhere. Leadership qualities are very much part of an individual's character, though there are ways to develop and improve your own leadership style. Leadership may be seen as a package of skills which can be learned.

Leadership and management

Leadership is part of management. It is often thought that leadership and management are the same thing, but there is a difference. Management involves organising resources (including people) towards achieving business goals, while leadership involves influencing the behaviour of people to achieve those goals. Leaders must attend to the details of carrying out management plans.

Types of leadership style

Different theories identify different types of leadership style. There are three main styles of leadership, though an adept leader can select and use the style which suits a particular occasion.

Authoritarian

Authoritarian leaders have a high degree of direction and control over their group. Generally, they give out orders which they expect to be obeyed without question. An authoritarian leader allows little, if any, participation from the group in decision making. This style produces a high level of work when the leader is present – though productivity falls when the leader is absent. There is a high degree of group dependence on the leader and little chance for staff to show their initiative. The group seem to accept the authoritarian approach, though dissatisfaction often shows in other ways (eg a high level of grievances or high staff turnover). Some members of the group may rebel against this style of leadership.

Democratic

Democratic leaders involve members of their group in most levels of decision making. As well as allowing the group to discuss action to be taken, the democratic leader often allows participation in decisions on policy. This style of leadership produces a steady level of work at all times. It facilitates friendly and interpersonal relationships and the group is more positive towards the leader. There is a greater acceptance of change amongst the group along with lower absenteeism and a higher level of job satisfaction. There is a degree of cohesion among the group although individual differences are not stifled.

Laissez-faire

Laissez-faire leaders basically let their teams get on with things without giving directions. The leader may provide information at the group's request but makes few decisions, resulting in the group being chaotic and confused. This can encourage conflict and frustration within the group and lead to group members questioning the leader's authority.

Leadership skills

There are three main skills which may be found in the successful leader.

Diagnosing skills

Diagnosing enables leaders to understand situations which they wish to influence. A leader must understand the present situation and must know what is expected or required in the future. The action necessary to achieve or prevent that future can then be taken.

Adapting skills

Adapting involves adjusting your behaviour and resources to enable the group to achieve its goals. Leaders must adapt both their own behaviour and the behaviour of other group members.

Communication skills

Communication involves passing information, ideas and instructions in a way which people can easily understand and accept. For the group to understand and accept the present and expected situations the leader must communicate effectively. Failure to do so means

that either the problem may not be solved or
the solution will not have the impact intended.

Working with people

People have been characterised as either lazy,
avoiding responsibility, and having to be coerced
into making an effort for the company, or as
applying self-direction to put a natural effort into
their work, seeking responsibility, and having
unused potential. In reality, individuals cover a
spectrum from one extreme to the other.

Relationships

Every leader must manage relationships
between the leader and the group as a whole,
the leader and individual members of the
group, and, to some extent, between group
members. A leader should try to assess the
character of each group member and establish
what makes each of them tick. In this way the
leader should be able to relate to each group
member. Communicating with the group and
individuals is very important in managing the
relationships. A leader should provide feedback
about situations and progress.

Motivation

The ability to motivate staff is a key element of
leadership. To motivate others it is important to
be motivated yourself. A leader's own behaviour

is an important influence on those around them. There are various techniques that can be used to motivate your staff. Recognise the efforts of others – people like to be appreciated. Routine praise is ineffective – praise must be done in a natural way and should be genuinely meant. Giving people responsibility will also motivate them as long as they are not overloaded. Simple changes in the working environment provide motivation if staff see them as an attempt to improve their conditions.

Empowerment

Empowerment is about getting the people who work for you to take responsibility for the tasks they are given – often key business functions. If you empower people to perform a task you must also give them the authority required to get the task done. Empowerment can be used to develop and motivate staff. Look for opportunities to use empowerment. It can be used when you have too much work, too little time and most importantly when a particular member of staff has special skills which suit a particular task. When empowering someone to do a job: discuss the task, set targets (eg completion dates), offer support, monitor progress and review their performance with them when the task has been completed.

Fairness

It is important that the leader is seen to be fair to all staff. This involves setting people targets which are not too low or too high and sharing out responsibilities. Fairness should encourage staff to take difficult decisions more readily and reduce conflict with the group. If group members suspect another member is receiving preferential treatment, motivation suffers and resentment against the leader and that member arises.

Developing leadership skills

Aim to develop and improve your own style of leadership. To do this you first need to identify and assess the strong and weak areas in your existing skills and knowledge. Training and development can then be used to improve the weak areas.

Leadership skills develop more through practice than theory, although learning the theories of motivation and communication will help. Programmes which improve the human aspects of leadership (such as communicating) are particularly important because most people are not as strong on these skills as they like to think. Other skills to be developed include planning, prioritising, anticipating problems, monitoring progress, and crisis management.

There are several methods that you can use to develop your leadership skills.

Fly-on-the-wall

This involves sitting in with someone known to be a good leader and watching how they work – usually over several short sessions. Observation is complemented by discussing what happened and how the leader handled each situation and problem.

On-the-job development

This involves developing skills by leading a group – using existing experience and knowledge, and advice from others, to solve problems. Feedback on performance should be provided by observers and group members. The group should also discuss their own and the leader's expectations, needs and concerns. The method is also called collaborative or 'synergistic' learning.

Achievement objectives

This method is often used with the fly-on-the-wall method or on-the-job development. It involves the leader and an adviser setting objectives to be achieved. As well as quantifiable objectives, aims such as reducing conflict within the group can also be set.

Leadership development workshops

A number of leaders attend regular meetings – usually with a training provider (eg a business school). In these meetings each member will discuss their activities since they last met and receive feedback from the other leaders on their performance. The meetings can be used as a vehicle for identifying the leaders' strengths and weaknesses and also to arrange training.

Case studies

This involves leading a group through a simulated 'realistic' business situation. This allows the leader to develop practical leadership skills without being 'on-the-job'. The leader is observed and receives feedback on performance.

Outdoor activity training courses

These courses are usually held in remote locations. The leader takes a group through various tasks, often with minimal equipment. The leader is forced to co-ordinate the suggestions and activities of the group members and to think on his/her feet. Progress is usually monitored and a feedback session conducted.

- *Aim to develop your own leadership style – seek training if you need it. Know what you want to achieve.*

- *There is no one best way to lead. Try different methods to find out which best suits you, your staff, particular situations and the business – but always establish who is in charge. The quality of your leadership depends on the methods you use to motivate others.*

- *Communicate with your staff; in particular, learn to listen. Let them know what you expect of them. Find out what they think is expected of them. If opinions differ find out why. This will reduce conflict, improve motivation and enable the group to make progress.*

- *Pay attention to your employees' working environment; comfortable chairs and decent lighting will show that you take their needs seriously.*

- *Try to build a good relationship with your staff inside and outside work.*

- *Expect others to be self motivated, but do not count on it.*

● *Given a clear idea of what needs to be done and why, most people perform well if they are given a degree of freedom and/or consultation on how results are to be achieved and a chance to vary their tasks.*

● *Try to be firm, neither too harsh nor too soft, and fair. Do not discipline staff publicly and never insult or humiliate them.*

7 Managing growth

This section considers managing the growth of
a small business.

Introduction

All businesses pass through stages of growth. It
occurs for a number of reasons: changes in the
commercial market; increased customer demand
for services or products; higher numbers of
customers, etc. Growth usually also occurs
when the management wish to actively expand
the business. Some plan to grow their businesses
indefinitely, others prefer to limit growth to
maintain control and involvement in the day-to-
day processes of running the business. The
manager must be aware of the implications of
growth and integrate its management into the
overall approach to the business.

The business growth life cycle

Levels of growth fluctuate depending on various
external influences. Change can occur at any
stage, if only to ensure survival. The small
business with a positive commitment to growth
is more likely to succeed in the long term. The
successful small business changes continually.
Growth may be rapid, steady, or in fits and starts,

but tends to follow the four stages outlined below:

1 Birth – seeking out finance for start-up costs, building a customer base, settling into premises, hiring staff and developing goodwill

2 Survival – problems at this stage include obtaining a niche market, staff development, product refinement, establishing internal systems, and determining staff roles and lines of control. The business gradually becomes more stable as it moves to stage three

3 Growth – the customer base, internal systems, staff and company resources expand while the business's products become more refined and diversified

4 Diversifying management control, delegation of key tasks, formalised management procedures and planning for business succession.

Stage four may involve continuing growth, or survival, or decline, depending on the firm's success or failure in stages 1 - 3. Each stage presents different challenges.

Different types of business growth

Growth means different things to different firms. Rapid growth can create problems as, typically, all management issues are heightened and individuals find themselves under greater pressure. Growth can take many different forms:

- Location – the business may have to expand spatially, perhaps buying new premises, adding to existing buildings or establishing another branch of the business elsewhere.

- Sales – expansion may be in the area of sales and profitability. You may establish higher sales targets or try to reduce costs.

- Geographically – growth may involve targeting customers from a wider area.

- Diversifying existing products – the introduction of new or revised products in response to customer needs, or to target new customers.

- Increased staff levels – this can enlarge production capacity and provide more time for strategic management/marketing tasks, etc.

- Importing and/or exporting – the Single European Market has made trade between EU countries easier.

- Greater demand for products – requiring the business to grow in one or more of the above ways.

Managing growth

Managing growth requires a knowledge of change management and an awareness of the implications of expansion for the business.

Strategic planning for growth

Ideally, the expansion of a business requires long term strategic planning. However, small firms often find that they do not have the time to develop such plans. This is because the managers are deeply involved with the day-to-day running of the business. Stable operations often get away with this, but in conditions of growth, the lack of a systematic planning process can be disastrous. Good business planning brings growth and increased profitability in times of boom, and aids survival in the lean years.

A plan for growth should balance investment and costs on the one hand, with cash and profit generation on the other. Planning is important to all areas of a business. Developing sales must be matched by increased capacity to meet new commitments. Planning needs to consider the short term as well as the long term, as circumstances vary daily. The planning process should involve everyone and should also look at the approach which individuals take to their time management. The everyday discipline of foreseeing changing circumstances and deciding how to deal with them is fundamental.

There is no single planning approach that can be applied to all small firms. A strategic plan includes goals for marketing, finance, staff development, etc, and proposes the time schedule for each objective. The objectives should be clear and specific. A strategic plan may also include other relevant subjects such as quality, diversification, acquisitions, market share improvement, sales growth, etc.

The management of change

Managing growth within a business requires skills in change management. There will be changes in responsibilities and lines of management. Managers will delegate tasks, and new systems and procedures will be set up. A strong management team and organisational structure will be needed to accommodate the firm's growth.

Organisational change often causes employee anxiety over job security and career opportunities. It is advisable to brief staff on possible changes before they happen. The key is to replace uncertainty with information in order to deter misconceptions. An open forum for communication is important.

Training must be provided for all employees, particularly if growth brings significant job changes. Encourage employees to evaluate and improve systems as needed. Provide employees with adequate support, as well as clear organisational roles.

The organisation as a whole has to be prepared for productivity to drop during change. Employee self-esteem and organisational energy will decrease. Eventually though, change should have a positive effect on the organisation.

Practical implications of growth

The management of growth at a strategic level is extremely important, but it is also useful to understand the practical implications of expanding your business.

Hiring new employees

Moving from operating as a sole trader to a partnership or an employer is a difficult step to take. However, if the business is to grow, it may be an essential progression.

Hiring employees is expensive. When considering cash flow, take into account the costs of recruitment, training, pension contribution, employee liability, national insurance, taxes, health and safety regulations, and personal records, as well as the cost of a salary. Be selective about who you hire. Make sure they will fit in with the other employees. Employee dissatisfaction results in low quality products, an unpleasant atmosphere and general disruption to the flow of business.

The hiring of employees inevitably rids the entrepreneur of many of the more mundane business tasks. There will also be some loss of direct involvement with the day-to-day running of the business. Some owners do not like becoming 'the boss'. Entrepreneurs have to learn to delegate tasks and relinquish control of some business operations in order to create the capacity for growth. The recruitment of appropriately skilled individuals, who are trustworthy, reliable and dedicated to the job, is important. Success depends on the efforts of others, not just the entrepreneur's motivation.

An alternative to hiring more employees may be to bring in a partner. Before establishing a partnership, you will need to decide exactly how responsibilities will be split and how soon the partner will have full business control. It is particularly important that you completely trust and feel able to work with the new partner.

Consider subcontracting some work if you are reluctant to employ people directly. It is important to assess the firms to whom you intend to subcontract work. An irresponsible company will damage your reputation. Subcontracting may also be a way to increase your customer base, especially if the subcontract firm offers parallel goods or services to your own.

Relocation

Many small firms are initially run from small, low cost premises – often the home. As the business expands, so will the work area needed. For some idea of what to expect, consider how expensive it is to move house. For a firm to open additional branches, considerable strategic planning is needed to ensure success. The owner/manager should be concerned not only with site selection, financing and staffing, but also with the degree of independence each site will have and the adequacy of information and accounting systems.

Increasing efficiency

To deal with the challenges of growth it is essential to run a tight, well designed operation. If you need to increase capacity, make sure you allow plenty of time to test out new systems and products and ensure that they work properly. It is all too easy for costs to get out of control.

Ensure you invest in suitable cost control systems as you increase capacity – you may need help to do this. Are you working to optimum efficiency? There is no point expanding inefficient systems into bigger ones. Use the principles of Total Quality Management to ensure you are running an efficient operation.

Teleworking

Teleworking may be an appropriate way to deal with growth. Having employees working from home reduces the pressure on space, decreases overheads, and keeps the office size to a minimum.

Legal implications of growth

The legal aspects of growth depend on the circumstances of the firm and its stage of growth. Possible legal considerations for a young firm as it expands in some manner will include one or more of the following:

- Will the form or status of the business change? For example, moving from a sole trader to a partnership, registering as a limited company, or becoming an employer

- Will the authorised share capital or the Memorandum of Association change?

- Will the nature or form of contracts entered into change?

- Will the methods of selling and distribution change?

- Will a new product or process be introduced?

- Will the insurance position change?

- *Ensure all aspects of the business operation are integrated into the overall plan for growth. Limit your plan to what you can realistically deliver.*

- *Decide once and for all if you really are committed to further business growth. Do you prefer working in a small operation? Are you prepared to deal with the challenges of increased responsibility?*

- *Learn how to develop and manage a larger working team. Implement systems and introduce expertise to ensure you can manage your staff properly.*

- *Ensure that you can fund all aspects of the operation in order to increase capacity. If you cannot, limit your objectives.*

● *Get professional support to help manage growth – including management consultancy, business advisers and accountants. If you encounter serious problems seek help immediately.*

Management
issues

8 Total Quality Management

This section gives an insight into Total Quality Management (TQM) and the benefits of implementing a TQM culture into any business, regardless of size.

Introduction

Total Quality Management is a culture within an organisation which brings about continuous improvement, through prevention of problems rather than the solving of problems once they have occurred. TQM is a methodology of quality awareness involving everyone within your business in customer focus and the need for quality.

Why TQM?

TQM should be adopted because it is an opportunity for your business to improve in all departments and areas of practice. The benefits of quality improvement include cost savings, staff involvement and responsibility for their own work, and a feeling of belonging.

Through staff involvement at all levels of the business, people become keen to do their job right first time, every time (which after all, is what you are paying them to do). This leads to reduced rework, reduced scrap levels, improved customer supply levels, an enlarged customer base and ultimately customer confidence in you, encouraging expansion of the business.

British business has always been heavily involved in 'firefighting' as problems occur without ever receiving a permanent solution. TQM is a method of preventing the fires starting, allowing managerial skill to be used in developing the business, and addressing problems as they arise with a permanent solution so that they cannot resurrect themselves.

Key principles of TQM

Management commitment and quality policy

Within your business it is imperative that TQM is driven down through the business from the Managing Director, with you showing constant visible support to the concepts of TQM. You must therefore have a clearly defined quality policy to show commitment and give an indication of the importance you place upon quality within your company.

An example of a quality policy would be as follows:

'Our policy is to provide products and service of the highest quality which fully satisfy our customers' requirements. Total Quality will be a permanent feature within this company. It will be implemented, monitored, nurtured and maintained by having a continuing quality improvement programme, which will be achieved through our people working together for success.'

It is vital however that all the managers within your business are totally committed to the concepts of TQM, because if any scepticism is seen by the workforce then they will not become committed to it. If the culture change then fails it will be very difficult to raise TQM as an issue in the future.

People aspects of TQM

People aspects of TQM involve all the people working within your business. No-one must be excluded.

The people within the business must first accept that quality is their responsibility, regardless of their position. Quality cannot be inspected into a product. It must be built in at the planning stage. Inspection can only weed out the defective material and is not 100%

effective. Some defects will always be missed even if only through human error.

Once the people of the organisation have accepted that they are responsible for the quality of the product or service they supply, then they should be actively involved in trying to bring about improvements in their own area of work. After all, they are the experts at what they do; they do it eight hours per day. This can be done in a number of ways. One is a suggestion scheme; another is the use of improvement teams to identify problems and develop solutions.

Small but continuous improvements within the business are of great benefit as they keep the process moving in manageable steps. All improvements made must be rewarded with recognition of a job well done. This reward does not necessarily have to be monetary. Often a 'well done' from the boss is sufficient.

Teamwork is also an extremely important aspect of TQM. It allows interaction between employees and can be extended across departments with the use of improvement teams.

Quality techniques

There are numerous quality techniques which can be employed. The most productive are listed overleaf with some possible applications:

a) **Quality costing**

This allows a cost of quality to be calculated for the business. The cost of quality includes failure costs (those incurred through failure such as seconds and rework), preventative costs (costs due to putting actions into place which will prevent a failure), and appraisal costs (such as testing prior to despatch to ensure that the specification has been met). It has been shown that in businesses which have not undertaken a quality improvement programme such as TQM the cost of quality on average is between 10% and 40% of turnover.

Quality improvement reduces failure costs, and the need for some appraisal costs, by an increase in preventative costs. Each improvement must be evaluated to ensure that the preventative cost encountered outweighs the appraisal and failure cost, but any improvement, however small, is a saving in terms of the cost of quality to the business.

b) Problem solving techniques

Brainstorming allows the involvement of a number of people (ideally approximately six), to identify the possible causes of a problem encountered within the business. Within the brainstorming process the participants are encouraged to allow their thoughts to run wild and record all comments. This may show up a number of causes not normally considered. It also encourages teamworking.

'Pareto analysis' is a process of allowing the most common causes of a problem to be identified and hence targeted for improvement. It was Pareto who showed that 20% of the causes of a problem produce 80% of the effects.

Cause and effect analysis (fishbone diagrams) encourage a logical thought process to enable potential causes of the problem to be assigned, identified and targeted for improvement.

c) Statistical process control

This is a technique by which a process can be maintained and controlled. It allows us to identify whether a process or machine is capable of manufacturing consistently to the tolerances placed upon it. It also allows monitoring of the process, thus identifying when it is going out of control and enabling corrective measures to be put in place with the minimum of delay.

d) **Quality engineering**

This encourages quality to be considered at the design stage, and is often done through failure mode effect criticality analysis (FMECA). This technique gives the ability to assess any failures which could occur within the process. By identifying possible failures which could occur, and identifying the impact the failure would have on the process, it is possible to eliminate the most critical causes of problems before the process even begins.

Quality system

A quality system within a TQM culture is seen to be central as it offers procedural methods of operation and defined standards of workmanship. The system then acts like a wedge to maintain any quality improvement made, preventing things slipping back to the way they were prior to the improvement. A recognised quality system will conform to the ISO 9000 series.

Introducing TQM to a company

There is no single method of introducing TQM into a company. Each individual company has its own requirements depending upon its current culture and quality awareness. Several people have given methods of TQM implementation defining steps of development as follows:

- Understanding of TQM

- Commitment and policy

- Organisation for quality improvement

- Measurement of the cost of quality

- Planning the quality improvement programme

- Designing the quality improvement programme

- Quality systems development

- Capability studies of current processes

- Control of current processes

- Teamwork

- Training

- Implementation of the total quality management culture.

The 12 points previously listed will of course be on a continuous cycle of: *plan, do, check, act*, even when a TQM culture has been achieved.

Training

Training is the key to TQM implementation and should be the largest aspect of any TQM implementation budget. Staff require training in:

- The concepts of TQM

- Increasing awareness of TQM within the business

- The use of quality techniques

- The use of quality systems

- Teamworking.

Training is a continuous process within a TQM culture ensuring that staff have the knowledge and skills required to carry out the tasks asked of them.

USEFUL TIPS

- *Be patient. A TQM culture change is a long process regardless of the size of organisation.*

- *Ensure that commitment is shown from the top down.*

- *Visible commitment should be shown by the managing director.*

- *Use the following six areas as a central focus for everyone:*

  - *TQM involves everybody*

  - *Always consider the elimination of waste, 'get it right first time, every time'*

  - *Customers must come first, both internal and external*

  - *Systems and procedures must become core to everything you do*

  - *Always look at ways of reducing the cost of quality*

  - *TQM is 'continuous improvement'.*

9 **Information management**

This section looks at the management of information within a business.

Introduction

It is essential for management decisions to be based on appropriate information. Managers need to know about employee performance, and how the business is performing, if they are to control and improve operations adequately. Information about competitors, markets and technology is essential for strategic planning. Too often information is gathered and used in an ad hoc fashion. Information can be inadequate, or there can be far too much of it. Some businesses are more 'information critical' than others. It helps to see information management as a distinct function, to budget for it and to manage it in order to achieve maximum effectiveness. Big companies reach a high level of sophistication in this area, but even small operations will benefit from a more systematic approach.

Evaluating information

Information should not be confused with data. A list of figures means little without explanation.

To be useful, data must be turned into information by analysing it and presenting it in a form appropriate to the user. Managers should be able to delegate the evaluation of information. The person responsible should have the discretion to make decisions about what is important, and should have the skills to present it in a way that can easily be understood. Some information must be kept by law for set periods of time. Failure to do so may result in prosecution.

Information for management

In smaller businesses, managers stay aware of market conditions through their daily contact with customers and suppliers. As the business grows managers become ever more distant from the grass roots and do not have immediate access to this basic information. A senior manager may be too busy to check personally on every aspect of the operation, but still needs to know what is happening in order to take valid strategic decisions. There comes a time when a separate information resource should be introduced to the business.

Information for other staff

This should be on a 'need to know' rather than a 'nice to know' basis. Often people want as much information as possible, associating information with power. Information overload can be counter productive – causing people to miss something really important. Prioritising information ensures the focus is on the most important things, but also helps keep the information management process economic. A good rule of thumb is not to collect information if you do not know how you are going to use it. Beware of keeping staff in the dark about the firm's activities – this can affect staff morale and may cause operational problems.

Information strategy

Information management is about finding a way to collect, handle and distribute information to the right people. Good information is relevant, accurate, and produced at the required time. Data must be collected, stored, analysed and presented to managers in an appropriate form. There should be a strategy to ensure that the correct information is received, and that any held is not kept too long but is not thrown out before legal requirements allow. It should ensure that the information is presented appropriately, and that it can be retrieved when the need arises.

Staff should be involved in developing the information strategy. Information gathering activities should be co-ordinated. In some firms people collect data independently and do not pass it on to colleagues. They may not realise its importance to other sections of the business or may be trying to protect their own jobs. If everyone realises the importance of information to the whole company, the strategy may be more successful. Produce a written document including objectives, policy, budgets, responsibilities and any other relevant documentation (eg lists of categories, request forms, etc). Ensure staff know how to use the system.

External information

- *Market intelligence.* Information about markets keeps you aware of future changes or trends and puts you in a better position to react. It is also useful to be aware of any general economic trends that may affect buying habits of companies and consumers. Market information helps in planning marketing or advertising campaigns as you will know the wants and needs of your customers. Forecasts based on inaccurate information will be incorrect.

- *Competitor information.* It is important to know what your competitors are doing, and any new products they may be in the process of launching. By knowing the prices that your competitors are charging you can tailor your promotions or modify prices accordingly. If you employ sales staff then they will be aware of competitor activity from talking directly to customers. Ask them to feed-back any relevant facts that they come across.

- *Legislation*. A thorough knowledge of current and forthcoming legislation, and how it affects your firm, is vital. If you do not comply with the law, you may suffer the consequences. There is also European legislation to consider.

- *Sales information*. Being aware of your sales figures is vital for maintaining production at the correct level. If you are working towards the 'Just In Time' (JIT) system then this type of information is extremely important as you do not want to hold too much stock, but must have enough to meet production demands.

Internal information

- *Financial information*. It is essential to know the financial position of the business; how and when it pays its bills and the length of time it waits to be paid. Costings of products will depend on knowledge of financial data.

- *Technical information*. Production targets can only be set with real accuracy if the current level of production is known. New technology can help improve production so it is vital to know what new equipment is available.

- *Employee information*. This can consist of basic personnel records, but it is useful to know the skills and potential available in your workforce.

Processing information

Procedures and methods should be devised to process information.

- *Evaluation and distribution*. Someone must be responsible for evaluating information coming in to the business, deciding whether to keep it or not, and providing it to the right person.

- *Indexing and storing*. The development of a system for categorising stored information is critical. Standard reference systems could be used or categories could be developed in consultation with all staff. If any information is confidential it should be clearly marked and kept in locked filing cabinets or be password protected on computer. Passwords should be changed regularly.

- *Searching and retrieving.* Equally, information must be retrieved quickly when it is needed. A computer database can speed up the process.

- *Acquisition and research.* The purchase of information must be co-ordinated to avoid duplication and control costs.

Computerisation

Many large companies now integrate all their information into computerised systems known as Management Information Systems (MIS). The aim is to provide managers with all relevant strategic information at the touch of a button. This requires an IT investment and expertise at a level normally beyond a small business. Nevertheless, IT and information skills are compatible and most internal information (see page 107) now tends to be computerised (eg accounts, customer databases, etc). Many small businesses try to integrate the two roles even if the external information remains paper based.

If installing a Management Information System, allow consultation between the IT specialists, the staff who will run the system, and those who will use the information it produces. If you rely heavily on IT, set up an emergency policy to enable vital information to be retrieved if there is a major computer failure. Computer data should be backed up and other copies of essential documents made. These should not be kept with the originals.

Dissemination

Presentation

Information is no use unless presented to the right person in the right format. It can be presented in many different ways, eg as a written report, as a table of figures, as a chart. It must be understandable. Quantitative reports can convey more detail than qualitative reports. 'Sales of product x are up by 75% this month' is more useful than saying 'sales of product x are good this month'. The nature of the information and the needs of the business will determine which approach is best.

Common information

Some information will be useful to everyone. This may be circulated on a routine basis to all employees. It can be worthwhile producing this as a newsletter – it imposes a discipline on what to circulate, and improves presentation. The information can be reused (eg for annual reports), and is useful for informing people outside the company (eg distributors, shareholders, partners, press, etc). Newsletter production should be budgeted for and controlled so as not to become an operational burden. Other information may be circulated to those on selected circulation lists.

Individual needs

Individuals within a firm will also have specific needs. This can get out of hand. People do not often appreciate that providing and managing information costs money. The person responsible should periodically review the information requirements of individuals (eg every six months). It can help to divide requirements into 'need to know' and 'nice to know'. The provider of information needs the discretion to say 'no' to requests, or to fix the amount that people receive.

Resources and management

Staff

One person should be made responsible for managing information in the business. How this is done depends upon the size and the type of the business concerned. Bear in mind that the business world is becoming ever more information intensive. There may be competitive advantage in recruiting someone with up to date information (and perhaps IT skills), to ensure that you benefit from the latest and best practice in information management.

Management

Lines of responsibility should be clear. Do not allow the role to be seen as a burden or as something to be done by whoever has a minute to spare. Information is a critical function. Management information can be sensitive. Information workers may need strong support from senior managers.

Budgets

Budgets should also be fixed. The way costs are allocated should be determined. Strategic information should be seen as a central function. Specific information costs may be allocated to particular projects or departments. Budget for staff costs, administration costs, overheads and IT costs. In particular there should be a set budget, shared between departments, for purchasing information (eg books, reports, periodicals).

USEFUL TIPS

- *Ensure that staff at all levels know the importance of information as a business resource.*

- *Information must be circulated to the right people, and in a useful format.*

● *Management information can be a sensitive issue. Be aware of this and try to ensure that the development of a system does not create internal political squabbles.*

● *Any information system you develop should be as simple as possible; if everyone can understand it, it is less likely to go wrong.*

10 Problem solving and business decisions

This section looks at problem solving methods with particular reference to business decisions.

Introduction

Problem solving and decision making methods are closely related. The need to solve specific problems occurs throughout the business operation. Decision making may be described as problem solving in the particular area of business strategy. Both involve a logical and systematic approach to define and analyse the problem, to generate possible solutions and to identify the best option.

Running a business is all about taking decisions. It is very tempting to take snap, 'instinctive' decisions. This is often necessary and sometimes very effective. All the same, such decisions can too often be the easiest, short-term option, which does not address the underlying problem. You may not have taken into account all the information available. Worse still, there may be others with more relevant knowledge which you can use, or who have already thought of an ingenious solution.

However good you may feel your instincts are, there is also a place for a more rational process to help you to identify solutions. Most problem solving methods are quite straightforward and involve nothing more sophisticated than paper, pencil and a little time for thought and discussion. Do not bang your head against a brick wall; use your intelligence to solve your problems.

Barriers

The first step in finding a solution is to recognise that a problem exists. The reaction to problems can often be to ignore them, to work harder (rather than smarter) or to find someone to blame. If you feel under pressure, tackling the problem itself can seem like the worst option. It is tempting to put it off for another time. Solving problems requires an investment of time. You may not feel that you have the time available. The problem may seem formidable. You may doubt your ability to come up with a solution. You may fear losing face if you get it wrong.

Do not prevaricate. If you have a serious problem the sooner you face up to it the better. If you have lots of problems, prioritise and tackle the most important ones first. Set aside time on a regular basis to think through your problems – this is a very important management function.

Make sure you will not be disturbed. Use a systematic approach. The problem solving process is designed to break things down and make them seem less formidable. Do not be afraid to ask you own staff for help, or to seek help from an external adviser.

The problem solving process

There is a well tried, logical framework for thinking through problems and coming up with solutions. The process is similar to the framework used in strategic documents such as business plans and reports. Whilst this might seem too involved for everyday use, the same basic approach can be applied to any problem, using paper and pencil. Often, a suitable solution will come up quite quickly, once you start thinking it through. If you are working alone use pencil and paper. If you are working in a group, use a flip chart.

Define the problem

What exactly is the problem? Pin it down exactly. The problem may not be what you first thought it was. Sometimes a solution can present itself at this early stage. How extensive, how important is the problem? Do you just need half an hour to think it through by yourself, or, do you need to call a meeting? Do you need to commission some research? If the decision affects others, do you need to seek their views before you put forward a solution?

Search for relevant information

Sketch out what you already know about the problem. Talk to your colleagues, and check your files to fill in the gaps. Do not forget to consult your own planning notes. You may have thought this through before. Do you have an ideas file, or a suggestions file to call on? Refer to your business plan; it should provide the strategic framework for most of your operational decisions. On a less formal level, talk to one or two colleagues and bounce ideas around. Is there a basic book or manual which might contain a straightforward solution to your problem?

Analysing information

Analysis is the process of breaking things down and giving them a structure that you can understand. It can often be quite a playful process where you put things in order and look for patterns. It helps you understand the problem better and should make it seem far less formidable. A very simple method is to list pros and cons for each option. It can be helpful to break down the information under headings. Any documentation you create may be useful for future reference. The journalist's six questions can be useful – what, why, when, how, where and who? Mapping out problems as flow charts or pattern notes is also useful. Again, discussion is very useful for working through ideas. Can you identify the critical areas which need the most thought and attention, which form the 'heart' of the problem?

Generate a range of options

Do not be tempted to go for the first idea that comes into your head. Set up a number of scenarios and look at the consequences of each. This is the stage where you need creative thinking. Use a brainstorming session (see over). Use the opportunity to involve others in coming up with solutions, especially the creative and imaginative people in your team. Try not to create false expectations that all their suggestions will be used.

Evaluate options and decide

Review your objectives. Look at each option critically. Which best meets your objectives? Can you balance this against the risks in each case? What are the cost implications? When you have weighed up the options, it is absolutely essential that you go on and take a decision. It is only worth setting aside time to solve problems if you are also prepared to set a time limit and commit yourself to a decision at the end of the process. Do not get stuck in 'paralysis by analysis'. You may not be entirely comfortable with your solution, but you have given it thought and now you must make a commitment. If it is a group decision, or a solution suggested by one person, give the decision your full backing. Do not discourage participation by blaming others if the solution does not work.

Quick decisions

Decisiveness is an essential leadership quality. Work teams look to their leader to take responsibility and act on their judgement. Decisions, if they are not to be random, need to be based upon a frame of reference. In order to decide, you have to know what it is you want from your business. If you do not have strong feelings about what you are doing, it will be difficult to take decisions about it. At the business level, a wider strategic awareness of your objectives and strategies provides you with the framework for your day to day decisions. If this is not clear, it will be hard to decide.

Even so, there are still many occasions when you do have to take snap decisions. This is all about confidence. On the whole, it is better to act than not to act. You can only judge your decisions by their results. You can only learn more about your business and what you want from it by taking decisions. The only way to improve your judgement is by constantly testing it out. Do not be tempted to act impulsively. If you are under stress or angry, you may do something stupid. Try to settle yourself and calm down before you start to think about solutions.

Brainstorming

Brainstorming is a well tried method of generating ideas. It is a relaxed approach which aims to get you to search out all the ideas lurking in the back of your mind. Brainstorming is normally done in a group. The aim is to create an atmosphere and momentum that throws up more and more ideas. You normally require a quiet room and a flip chart or white board to write down the suggestions. The session may be called to generate solutions, or the group may be involved in the whole problem solving process. However you approach it, it is important that the problem is well defined for the group before the session starts.

The group is then encouraged to come up with ideas. Everyone should realise that at this stage any idea, no matter how far fetched, is acceptable. It is a rule that no-one is allowed to criticise or mock unusual ideas. In fact 'way out' ideas should be encouraged (the person writing down the ideas should write down exactly what was suggested). This should create a relaxed 'fun' atmosphere where people are searching in their minds for anything they can think of to solve the problem. Sometimes the idea that at first seemed impossible is the best option. Usually the atmosphere of open minded discussion throws up an obvious solution which for some reason had been overlooked. It is important to set a time limit. Brainstorming should be followed by a critical analysis by the group of each idea. The best solutions should be identified and acted upon.

Problem solving in teams

Problem solving requires a combination of a logical and creative thinking. To an extent these are contradictory qualities, which is why it can be helpful to involve a number of people in the process. You may have a particular member of staff who is particularly good at problem solving. Use this person whenever you can. It is important to encourage an open-minded and trusting environment where everyone feels able to identify problems and suggest solutions. Using groups or teams to solve problems is certainly good practice and produces all sorts of fringe benefits. On the other hand, groups must be managed properly if they are to work effectively. Someone must be responsible for chairing the group, documenting results and commissioning research. Do not appoint a team if the problem does not warrant it or if the results are unlikely to be used.

● *After analysing a problem, it can help to allow time for your subconscious to work on a solution. Sleep on it.*

● *Taking decisions is the essence of management. Once you have given the matter due consideration, take the decision and stick to it. You will often feel uncomfortable and doubt that you have done the right thing. You will be criticised, and there will be times when you get it wrong. As a manager it is essential for you to accept the responsibility to trust your judgement and to take critical strategic decisions.*

- *Think about your own particular style of problem solving. What are the barriers which stop you addressing problems? What are your strengths and weaknesses when it comes to solving problems.*

11 Crisis management and disaster planning

This section considers some of the disasters and crises which can affect a business and explains how to minimise their impact through preparation.

Introduction

A crisis can be loosely defined as a sudden unexpected event that cannot be solved by normal procedures. Stress, created by the sudden change in circumstances, is always a factor towards making something a crisis. It can be difficult to define 'crisis' in detail because what is a crisis to one person may not be a crisis to another. A disaster is a very extreme form of crisis.

A crisis of any degree can have an adverse affect on a business, ranging from disruptive to devastating, depending upon the severity of the problem and how prepared the business is to cope. If not properly managed, a crisis can lead to loss of earnings, reduction in profits and ultimately, it may cause the business to go bankrupt. The damage caused by a crisis can, however, be minimised.

Types of crises

Crises can be classified into two main groups: external and internal. External crises are those which are outside the control of the business but which affect the business environment. External crises may include family problems or a bankrupt client leaving bad debts and order cancellations. More extreme examples of external crises are often classed as disasters, eg fire, flood, bomb alert, or explosion.

Internal crises are crises which occur within the business. They often have little or no effect on the external environment. Examples of internal crises include power or machinery failure, a computer crash, data corruption, or losing your diary, briefcase or filofax.

Minimising problems

Problems can be minimised before a crisis occurs, mainly through forward planning. You will need to devise and implement everyday business procedures to minimise the chances of a crisis occurring in the first place. You will also want to work out what you should do if any particular crisis does occur.

The important part of planning is to take time to identify the possible crises that may affect your business. Think through why they might occur and how you can prevent them from happening. Consider how they would affect you and what has to be done to put things right if they happen despite your precautions. It is much easier to think through all of the possibilities if you can involve other people.

The advantages of planning can be demonstrated by the 'torch principle'. If you are caught in a power cut at night, you will start to consider the possible causes of the power cut and will wish to investigate the ones that you can do something about. However, you cannot begin to investigate those causes, or do anything about putting things right, without first finding the torch. Trying to find a torch in the dark can be time-consuming, stressful and frustrating if you cannot remember where you left it. If you are prepared, having a specific place to keep the torch – and checking its batteries every month – then locating and using it in a power cut is easy.

Crisis management plans and teams

To avoid problems, every business should have a Crisis Management Plan (CMP). A CMP is a plan which details the action that should be taken in each given crisis situation. It may be detailed – describing the action to be taken by each individual, or it may be general – outlining areas of responsibility and procedures to be used. The CMP for each crisis should reflect the circumstances and the courses of action available. Even if a crisis is thought of as unlikely (eg an explosion), or unavoidable, it should be considered and planned for in order to minimise the damage caused.

To draw up an effective CMP the business should first conduct a crisis audit. This involves assembling all key staff to determine all the possible crises that may occur, as well as assessing the threat that each poses, no matter how insignificant or unlikely the crisis. For each crisis, a Crisis Impact Value (CIV) should be determined. This is done by asking five questions and allocating a score for each response. The questions to be asked in determining a crisis' CIV are as follows:

- How intense will the crisis get and how quickly will it happen?

- To what extent will the crisis be scrutinised by a body such as the government?

- How much will the crisis interfere with the day to day running of the business?

- To what extent will the business and your personal reputation be damaged by the crisis?

- What will be the level of damage to the business' bottom line?

Each response should be given a score ranging from 0 to 10. Low intensity, no scrutiny, minor interference, little damage to reputation and negligible effect on the bottom line should score 0. High intensity, close scrutiny, major interference, significant damage to reputation and a major effect on the bottom line should score 10. The five scores for each crisis should then be added up and the total sum divided by 5. This figure is the CIV. This process gives a numerical value to a crisis which can be used to determine its importance both on its own and in relation to other crises.

All possible actions, procedures, areas of responsibility, etc should be discussed to work out the best course of action in each given crisis. Generally, preparing a thorough CMP involves:

- Identifying the crisis

- Gathering all possible information about the crisis and the circumstances which may lead up to it

- Isolating the crisis

- Taking action to clear up the crisis and any damage caused by it.

A draft CMP can then be drawn up and tested. Once this has been done the plans should be written up in a document that is easily accessible by all relevant staff. The CMP should be regularly revised, particularly after a crisis, so that it can be improved.

Once a CMP has been drawn up the business should set up a Crisis Management Team (CMT) to deal with any crisis that occurs. A single person should be in charge of the CMT for decisions to be made more easily. It is the responsibility of the CMT to make sure that any actions, procedures, etc contained within the CMP are carried out. In the case of an external crisis they may be required to liaise with emergency services, government, media, etc.

Reacting to a crisis

When dealing with a crisis it is important not to panic because this can lead to hasty and incorrect decisions being made. To deal with a crisis efficiently and effectively there are a number of steps that should be followed:

Stop and think

First take a number of deep breaths as this will help stop any physical reactions. Collect and check all the facts before making any decisions.

Is there a CMP to cover the situation or any precedent to draw on?

Identify your objectives and priorities

Ask yourself what needs to be achieved, which are the most important factors and which issues need to be dealt with first.

Plan

Decide what needs to be done, by whom and in what order. This should be contained within the CMP for that particular crisis. However, ask yourself what else can be done; has the CMP missed anything?

Implement plans

Put someone in charge to make sure the CMP is followed and make sure that everyone knows who is in charge. Start taking the action specified in the CMP to clear up the crisis.

Communicate

Make sure that those people involved and who need to know what is happening (eg employees, customers) are informed about what has happened and what will be happening. Also make sure that the CMT keeps you informed if you are not part of the team.

Evaluate

Ask yourself how well the crisis was handled, what you would do differently next time, etc. If necessary change the CMP for future reference.

USEFUL TIPS

- *Evaluate your present systems and procedures.*

- *Identify all possible crises that may occur and determine a priority CIV for each crisis.*

- *Establish a Crisis Management Plan for each crisis identified. Keep copies of the plans at accessible alternative locations (at least one off-site – a crisis may destroy the original). Make sure everyone knows where the plan is kept, who has overall responsibility for implementing the plan and who is responsible for what action.*

- *Involve all staff in dealing with crises, even if it is just to let them know what is happening.*

- *Communication, both internal and external, is important in dealing with a crisis. It can allay fears and enable crises to be overcome more quickly, therefore limiting the damage caused by the crisis.*

- *Accept that there will always be un-certainty and insecurity in business and try to see crises as part of the learning curve and not as disasters.*

- *Each business should have a series of control systems and procedures that are followed carefully. These can include systematic recording of vital computer files on back-up disks to be kept off-site in case of data corruption, fire, etc; copies of vital documents kept off-site (or in a fireproof safe); appropriate levels of business insurance; clauses in contracts to protect against the cancellation of orders by clients; identifying a deputy; and ensuring that security systems work.*

12 Networking – managing business contacts

This section looks at the importance of making and keeping contacts to the success of a business, and outlines some basic ways in which a network of contacts can be built up and maintained.

Introduction

Networking is the term used to describe the active cultivation of useful contacts and the use of those contacts, when appropriate, to help in achieving required objectives. In most cases, those objectives are locating information and finding new customers.

Most people have heard of the 'Old Boy Network'. The term comes from public schools. Ex-pupils are known as 'old boys' and the schools encourage them to feel free to contact each other for mutual support, sometimes publishing directories of 'old boys', detailing their business positions and contact addresses. This creates a ready-made network, covering a wide range of business and professional fields.

It is unusual to be in the fortunate position of having a directory of willing contacts provided, but even without such a starting point, building a good network of contacts is something that can be achieved over time.

What makes a contact useful?

Contacts can serve several useful purposes. The most obvious is in providing direct or indirect links to potential customers. It is important not to think of this as their only function.

Research can be conducted through careful use of contacts to establish whether a market is viable in the first place. Whatever your position in a market you will want to be aware of any developments that might indirectly affect your business; a network can help here too. The right people can provide you with information about proposed changes in legislation in your industry, problems faced by customers or suppliers (or your customers' customers and suppliers' suppliers), etc that might have a knock-on effect on your business.

Building up a network

Networking is something that a lot of people do without ever thinking about it, but if it is carried out as a deliberate activity it is much easier to control the results. Chance encounters should never be ignored. Every conversation or introduction has the potential to provide useful contacts. It is not, however, a good idea to rely solely upon chance as a way of building a comprehensive network of business contacts. A methodical approach can be much more effective.

- *Think about why you want a network of contacts*. Is your priority to meet new customers or gather information? This is a question you should ask regularly because your priorities will change. Are there particular organisations that you wish to have a contact in?

- *Write out a simple plan of the contacts that you need to make, set yourself a schedule, and follow it systematically*. You may find that the first people you speak to are not in a position to give you the help you need. If this happens, be prepared to ask them for suggestions on who is the most appropriate person to speak to – and follow it up.

- *Seek out places where useful contacts might gather*. Your local enterprise agency may know of, or organise, an enterprise club. Enterprise clubs provide a relatively informal setting for people who run small businesses to get together socially, arrange entertainment and educational programmes, etc. Local Chambers of Commerce usually hold regular informal meetings for members, often based around informative talks followed by a buffet lunch. Don't be afraid to introduce yourself to people and discuss what both you and they do.

There may also be other fora which are specific to your industry or current business interests, eg regional branches of your trade association, professional institutions such as the Institute of Management, exporters' clubs, etc. These are usually designed specifically for the purpose of establishing contacts and exchanging information. Finally, don't forget any social or community activities in which you are involved. Organisations such as the Rotary Club have traditionally been seen as a fertile ground for networking purposes, but useful contacts may be found in many social scenarios.

- *Look for intermediaries who can make introductions*. The professionals that you deal with in business life are also dealing with other businesses. If you need to find contacts in a particular area try asking your accountant, solicitor or bank manager. Although they will be unable to discuss other clients in detail they may be able to make referrals.

If you are involved in any of the business counselling or training activities arranged by your local Business Link, enterprise agency, business school, etc, the trainers or counsellors involved will have a wide range of contacts themselves and will usually be willing to help their clients to get in touch with each other.

- *Don't forget friends – and friends of friends*. Most people have a variety of friends, relatives and acquaintances, who in turn have their own circle of friends, etc. Within this comparatively close set of relationships it is astonishing how often you know somebody who knows somebody who can help – the difficulty lies in making the initial connection.

- *Keep records of useful contacts*. A card index or personal organiser can be handy although many people will prefer to make use of a computer database instead of, or as well as, a paper based system. The sort of information you store depends on how methodical you are and how good your memory is. The basic details are name and phone number; but organisation name and address will also be essential in most cases. You can record things like contact dates and notes about what was said. Some people keep a note of information such as hobbies, names and ages of children, etc as memory joggers and to add a personal note to subsequent conversations.

Maintaining a network

Aim for a core of around seven or eight key people with whom you constantly exchange information. In addition, keep regular contact with the rest of your main contacts – you will have to determine the frequency appropriate to each. Many people make use of fax or e-mail to maintain their networks; regularly circulating relevant information between contacts. Some contacts can be noted down for future reference without a need to keep in touch. Inevitably, such contacts are more likely to fall out of date, but if you didn't need to get in touch with them for a long time you haven't wasted any effort.

A computer database should allow you to keep up-to-date on contacts by sorting the records by the date you last saw them. You can also use key words (eg customer, press, law, advice, training) to identify certain types of contact for later reference. Because a card index is not easily re-sorted, once you have decided on an order to keep the cards in you are fairly well stuck with it. Some flexibility can be introduced by colour coding cards to classify types of contact.

Organisations change and people move on. Keeping regular contact will hopefully mean that you are aware in advance of any changes and have had the chance to review your network in time to avoid finding that an important relationship with an organisation has been lost and must be built again from nothing.

USEFUL TIPS

● *It is quality, not quantity, that counts. A carefully selected network is easier to keep in touch with.*

● *Communication is the key; if you let people know what you are doing, what sort of information you need, etc they will be better placed to help you than if you keep yourself to yourself.*

● *Be prepared to work at networking. If you want to get the most out of it you have to put a lot into it. If you expect people to feed you information you should be* prepared to feed information to others. If you are in the habit of passing news on without being asked, others might learn to do the same for you.

● *Don't expect immediate results, good relationships need to be built up.*

● *Always remember that you are dealing with people. If you keep a relationship on a business only footing, and both parties treat it as such, there should be few problems. Similarly, if a close friend is in a position to help you they may well do so – not always relying on the principle that you will return the favour as appropriate. If, however, you regularly lean on friendship as a way of getting what you want, and never put anything back into the relationship, you are likely to find that your network starts to close down on you.*

● *Younger business people and those just starting out may find it useful to seek out – or to form – organisations targeted specifically at them. For example, many Chambers of Commerce and professional groups run networking and social events for junior or newly qualified members.*

- *If you keep personal information about your contacts on a computer, you should make sure that you comply with the Data Protection Act 1984.*

- *Keep a file or scrap-book in which to place any business cards you are given, and always put them in it when you return to the office; that way they don't get lost.*

Business
and legal
issues

part
three

13 **Franchising your business**

This section details the main areas to investigate when considering the development of a franchise network.

Introduction

Franchising allows a proven business idea to be sold as a ready-made business package to local operators in return for fees and other income. It provides a means to expand an operation rapidly without taking on all the responsibilities of ownership and management. Well established franchises include McDonalds, Prontaprint, The Body Shop, Dyno-Rod, Thrifty Car Rental, ServiceMaster, etc.

Some franchisors already own a well established business which they wish to expand. For others, a new product or service may have been developed within the business which they wish to distribute on a wider basis. Some franchisors start a business idea from scratch to develop into a franchise project. Turning a business into a franchise is a highly speculative venture which, whilst offering potentially substantial returns, also carries considerable financial risk.

Advantages

Franchising an operation can offer a number of advantages over developing the business yourself.

- An expanding business brings with it the operational difficulties of managing and motivating staff. A self-employed franchisee is normally strongly motivated to make their business a success because of their independence and stake in the enterprise. This should result in a better service for the customer

- Outlets may be expanded more quickly, due to extra capital supplied by the franchisees

- The franchisee is more likely to understand his/her local market

- Increased sales volume allows bulk purchase discounts

- The project is more likely to be supported by banks, as a lower risk is associated with franchise schemes

- It may be easier to expand internationally.

Disadvantages

- The initial start up costs of a franchise scheme are frequently very high and may not be recovered for a number of years

There is also the risk that the franchise is shown to be unworkable leaving you with the development costs to pay off

- There is less direct control over the network. Franchisees may not be trustworthy and may not disclose the extent of their success

- Franchisees may use the scheme to gain valuable knowledge and experience which they could use later to compete against you

- After the initial enthusiasm franchisees may reach a stage where it may be difficult to motivate them any further.

What can be franchised?

An operation must include distinct features to be a viable franchise prospect.

- If the operation is unique in some way in terms of product or image, it will offer a competitive advantage

- It must be possible to identify a clear gap in the market

- The skills involved in delivering the end product or service must lend themselves to standardisation throughout the network

- Products and processes must be able to be standardised throughout the network

- A range of suitable franchisees must be available

- The business must have a high turnover or high gross margin.

Finance

Investment costs

The initial outlay for the franchisor is usually high. Depending on the size of the planned project, it may take some time to recover the investment. Various stages which must be considered concerning financial costs are:

a) Initial costs eg market research, professional fees to consultants, accountants etc

b) Development costs including training courses, producing information packs, commissioning materials etc

c) Recruitment costs may also be quite high, covering initial advertising and promotional costs.

Costs will vary according to many factors eg type of business, degree of change required, etc.

Income

The franchisor receives the initial franchise fee, plus regular service fees which could take a number of forms, eg a percentage of turnover, a mark up on materials supplied, or a fixed minimum fee in addition to these.

Potential franchisees

Franchisees cannot be profiled too precisely. A franchise network will stand or fall on the quality of the people it recruits. The requirements will depend partly upon the type of activity involved. They must be prepared to invest capital in the project. A simple one person operation might only require a certain level of vocational skill eg, plumbing, joinery etc. If the franchisor will need to employ others, this will require some management experience. The franchisee clearly needs to be independent, resourceful and hard-working. On the other hand, franchisees must not be too independent, as they may start to resent the franchisor placing controls over them.

Other points to consider include:

- Is the potential franchisee suited to self-employment and the implications associated with it?

- Are their financial resources adequate for the project?

- The franchisee should be quite ambitious, but not to the extent that they resent some level of control

- The personal relationship between the franchisor and franchisee must be successful, mutual trust is essential.

Suitable franchise candidates will include people with proven skills who have capital available to invest.

The British Franchise Association

The BFA was set up in 1977 to represent the franchising industry and to develop professional standards of operating. There are three membership classifications. 'Full members' must have successfully run a pilot scheme for one year or more and must have at least four franchisees, two of which should have been going for two years. An 'associate member' must have run a pilot for one year and at least one outlet must have been running for over a year. Lastly, a 'provisional member' will be currently developing their franchise concept and taking accredited professional advice on its structure. All members must abide by the Code of Ethics. The BFA is a valuable source of support and information. It receives thousands of enquiries from potential franchisees. Membership is a powerful marketing aid for a franchisor, and will certainly be essential in persuading people to back you financially.

Other support

The development of a franchise network is highly technical and requires expertise in various areas. It is unlikely that a person new to business will possess all of these skills. They therefore need to seek professional support.

- Qualified franchise consultants are widespread in the UK, offering help with feasibility studies and business plans. They will advise on funding the development and in particular on promoting and recruiting the network

- A specialist solicitor will be essential in the production of a franchise agreement to control the network, contracts with consultants, etc

- Accountants are often required to assist in the preparation of financial statements. The BFA holds lists of its Affiliate Professional Members, which can be made available to you.

Develop the plan

To manage the development of the franchise package a comprehensive working business plan should be used. The plan will also form the basis of any funding applications you need to make. The plan will include:

- A description of the current situation

- Results from market research

- Results from a feasibility study

- Financial projections

- Proposed marketing methods for product /service

- Detailed description of operations.

Pilot study

The operation should be tested in a pilot study for at least one year before it is actually sold as a franchise. The study should aim to:

- Test the transferability of skills, ie how easily the skills, concepts and basic knowledge can be conveyed to the potential franchisee

- Test the success of the chosen location

- Test the compliance with legal areas

- Test the market reaction to products /services

- Identify any problems and enable the franchisor to make appropriate alterations, hopefully saving long-term costs

- Identify training needs

- Experiment with some variations on the basic theme

- Provide a variety of information which is required for production of the operations manual.

Setting up the franchise

With the evidence derived from the pilot study you should be able to decide if the operation will work, and obtain any further finance necessary to set it up.

- A franchise agreement must be drawn up with the aid of a solicitor to include items like opening hours, sources of supply and pricing policy

- You must provide a manual detailing all aspects of the operation, to assist the franchisee in running the operation and to help assure consistent standards

- Support services to the franchise network must be established. You will need premises, employees, equipment, working capital etc. An essential support element will be any national advertising activities in support of local franchisor advertising. This will require a carefully designed image and promotional strategy

- A training package must be developed to transfer effectively all the information and skills

- A control system is required to enable you to monitor the performance of the franchisees

- Job descriptions must be prepared before recruitment begins throughout the network

- Trained staff must be recruited prior to the setting up of the network and to act as a central control for new franchisees

- When the operation is fully developed take the appropriate steps to get legal protection for the package.

Launching the franchise

The way the franchise is launched, both to the public and to potential franchisees, will be critical. You will be aiming to establish a reputation quickly, and publicise the results in order to get more franchisees on board. Publicity will play a major part, including press releases, events, interviews etc. It may be necessary to employ a specialist marketing and PR agency to carry this out effectively. A variety of media may be used.

Franchisee promotion

Local and national press advertising including small ads, business and employment editorial coverage; trade and franchise media advertising /editorial (eg *Franchise World Magazine*);

franchise directories; trade/franchise exhibitions and shows.

Promotion to customers

National media advertising. Leaflet and brochures, PR, advertising guidelines, etc for use by the network.

USEFUL TIPS

- *The risks involved in a franchise project are substantial, but all operations are covered by your franchise agreement. It is essential that this agreement is thoroughly researched and covers every foreseeable aspect.*

- *Developing a franchise is a formidable project. It will be essential to establish close working partnerships with all the different agencies which can provide you with support.*

14 Common reasons why businesses fail

This section outlines some reasons why small businesses fail, and suggests ways to prevent or correct such problems.

Introduction

Businesses are at the greatest risk of failure in the first few years of trading. Chances of survival increase the older and more experienced a firm and its management become, even so, 50% of VAT registered firms fail within five years. It may take up to ten years for a business to stabilise. The main reason for the high failure rate of small, recently established firms is that the owner lacks experience in managing all aspects of a business at the same time. It is easy to be distracted by solving one problem and miss others until it is too late. A business must be kept in balance, even when it is growing rapidly. A manager must, for example, realise that a firm can fail as much through achieving too many sales as it can through too few sales. Most failure can be avoided if the right measures are taken.

Common reasons for failure

In surveys of small businesses, the biggest problems identified by owner/managers are:

- Lack of sales/low turnover
- Debtors/obtaining payment/cash flow
- Competition from bigger firms

Professional business advisers see things differently. They put the blame on poor management. Common complaints are:

- Businesses are often under-capitalised
- Managers believe that more capital would solve their problems, and don't address deeper seated issues
- They don't set and review targets
- They don't regularly monitor performance
- They don't take corrective action early enough
- They expect too much, too soon
- They view marketplaces as they want them to be, not as they really are.

They are *turnover* led instead of *profit* led

One survey showed that over 30% of failed firms had not sought advice from either their bank or their accountant before they went under.

Factors aiding success

It has often been shown that firms which seek professional advice and business skills training tend to do better than those that don't. The attitude of the owner, and work experience in the same business sector are also seen as helpful. Regular business planning can give a firm profit margins around 48% higher than those of firms that don't plan.

Where it goes wrong

Management

Owner/managers are usually specialists in the product or service their firm offers, or are very good at selling their product or service. However, they often lack the management skills needed to develop a strategy: business planning, training and managing people. Because of this, small businesses are often managed on a day-to-day basis and long term planning is neglected. In many cases, the owner-manager does not intend the business to grow, but simply to keep going. This can lead to business instability and employee insecurity. Owner/managers are very independent, this makes them less inclined to look for and accept advice from outsiders.

Finance

Financial difficulties are another major factor in business failure. The owners may have invested a lot of money in the business. This may include life savings, their home and other assets. Much depends on successful financial management of the business. The main problem financial areas for small firms include:

a) **Poor accounting and financial management**

Finances are often managed badly due to a lack of skill in this area. As with other management skills, the small business owner is rarely experienced in financial organisation.

b) **Cash flow and late payment problems**

If money flows into a business slower than it is paid out, the business has to rely heavily on its borrowing facilities. However, many small businesses have very little to spare, and they rely on their customers to be prompt with their payments to the business. This can affect the ability to pay suppliers, rent, rates, and wages, and to meet customers' requirements. Young businesses often fail to communicate their terms and conditions assertively when taking new orders, causing problems later on.

c) **Sales**

A business faces difficulties if sales aren't profitable. A common fault is pricing goods or services too low, forgetting that although the profit margin might look good, a lot of sales are required just to cover the overheads. Success can bring its own problems. When a business sells more products or services than its working capital facilities can cope with, it is in danger of overtrading, the result of which is having insufficient cash.

d) **Investment**

Beyond their own investment, most new firms rely heavily on their bank overdraft. Facing debts at start up is normal, but puts a strain on the business from day one. A number of loan schemes help people starting up in business, but financial assistance after the initial few months can be harder to find. As many new businesses face major problems in their first years, this can increase difficulties. A lot of small business owners avoid external financial input, feeling it limits their independence. Unfortunately, the stability and potential growth of the business can depend on the amount of finance available. Bank overdrafts can only ever be seen as short-term finance, so other options have to be explored.

Market

A number of external issues influence business success or failure. Markets can be unpredictable and potentially unstable. In some cases, the product may be inappropriate for the targeted customer group perhaps being too expensive or aiming at consumers who are simply not interested.

Need for training

Small firms often do not arrange training for managers or employees. Reasons include:

a) The manager and key staff can't spare the time

b) Training is seen as an unnecessary expense. Many managers believe they and their staff already have adequate skills for the job

c) It is felt that employees may use training as a route to another job.

Health or personal problems

Many small businesses are run almost single-handedly by owner-managers. This can easily cause problems when nobody can assist during times of stress, ill health or family problems.

Legislation

Complying with all appropriate legislation can be a major problem for the small business. The burden of filling in appropriate forms, staying aware of relevant legislation, etc. all put a strain on the business. Small businesses are subject to much the same requirements as larger firms, making administration costs higher in relation to business size. Occasionally, new legislation removes a market or makes it too costly to continue to serve it.

Preventing business failure

A well managed business can usually withstand most external and internal problems. Planning, target setting and performance monitoring will be included from the outset, and the management style will change as the business grows and develops.

Advance preparation

Before starting up, all risks should be considered. Are the potential rewards great enough? Some of the risks of setting up in business relate to external factors. The potential owner/manager should be aware of financial risks, problems of an unstable market, and legislation. They should also look at internal factors, assessing their potential as a manager, and determine whether they can work with the possible risks to themselves and their business. They should ask themselves a number of questions: 'Could I survive if the business failed?' 'Would I be able to cope with the stress brought upon me by the business?' and, 'How effective would I be at dealing with the problems of a small firm?'

Comprehensive discussions with an experienced business adviser before going into business can prevent a wide range of problems. Everyone affected by the decision to start a business should know exactly what will be required of them and what they will get out of it – this may call for discussions with family members.

Market research

Gaining credibility for a new business venture can be extremely difficult. Market research is important. It looks at what the business will do, what limitations it has, what products/services it offers and who requires them. A prosperous business depends on successful marketing to a target group of customers. Are there already a high number of businesses covering the area, or is competition minimal? How does the product/service offered differ from the competition? Without adequate market research, any number of problems can occur in these areas. Effective promotion of a service or product is also important. A marketing strategy based on comprehensive research can give a firm its best chance of success.

A comprehensive business plan

Business plans give details about the business idea, finance available, finance required, and potential return on investment. They draw heavily on market research by the potential owner/manager. A business plan helps show potential investors, bank managers, etc. the viability of the business. Its content and thoroughness is a guide to the business skills of the management. Once a business is trading, the plan can be used to monitor performance against targets and should be regularly updated.

Training

Training can really increase the survival chances of a small business. Many owner/managers know their product extremely well, but, in many cases, they don't know how to manage a business effectively. Adequate training for owners, covering management, marketing and personnel skills can cut out many of the problems of poor management faced by small firms. Giving training to employees increases their loyalty to the company whilst improving their capabilities. Staff training keeps them up to date with new developments and helps them to deal with changes in the business.

Managing the finances

To reduce cash flow problems, a business needs sufficient capital and back up resources to keep it financially stable. Very tight credit control is also important. This means keeping accurate and up-to-date accounts in a form which helps the management make informed decisions. Training in financial skills is readily available.

Facing business failure

The threat of business failure can be extremely traumatic. To manage the situation effectively, a manager should:

a)   Identify and tackle problems immediately

b)   Contact their business/financial adviser.

In many cases, a solution will be available, particularly in financial terms. Where banks are involved with the business, they will usually try to protect their investment. It is important for the owner/manager to maintain a positive attitude – and to remember that business failure does not make them a failure personally.

USEFUL TIPS

● *Seek advice wherever possible, many sources are free to small businesses.*

- *Before entering into a business, discuss possible problems and develop long term strategies to deal with them.*

- *If possible, in order to reduce personal financial risks, it is sensible to maintain an alternative source of income whilst getting the business established.*

- *To reduce potential problems, appoint a deputy. Make them aware of the plan or strategy to be used should the business manager be unavailable.*

- *Be aware of, and monitor, the potential business danger areas.*

- *Stay in touch with the marketplace and adapt to changing market requirements.*

15 Legal status of a business

This section describes the possible legal status that a business may choose.

Introduction

There are three types of legal status available to a new business. These are: sole trader, partnership and limited company. When determining which form of organisation is best for your venture, you should consider the implications of each status for your personal circumstances and the administration, finance and image of the business.

Sole trader

A sole trader (or sole proprietor) is a business in which one person is the owner. The business can, however, employ other people. Operating this way removes most of the formalities of establishing a business. There is no requirement to register as a sole trader, for example, although there are certain rules about the disclosure of ownership – see 'Business names' below.

At an early stage, contact should be made with the local Inland Revenue Office who will send out booklet IR28, 'Starting in Business', together with the appropriate form. All income is treated as personal income. Allowable expenses (ie most business expenses) are deducted to give a profit which is subject to personal income tax at the current rates. During the year, money is drawn from the business by the proprietor and is, therefore, called drawings. Drawings are simply an advance against profit. Accounts do not have to be audited although negotiations with the Inland Revenue will be easier if they are prepared by a professional accountant.

Contact should also be made with the Department of Social Security (DSS). Sole traders are required to pay Class 2 and Class 4 National Insurance Contributions at the current rates.

A sole trader is an unincorporated business, ie liability lies with the proprietor. A sole trader has 'unlimited liability'. This means that personal savings and assets could be at risk if the business fails, and the trader is made bankrupt. It is advisable to consult a solicitor with regard to the security of your personal assets. Equally, however, the sole trader takes all the profit.

Partnership

The Partnership Act 1890 defines a partnership as 'the relationship which subsists between persons carrying on a business in common with a view of profit'. Partnerships are neither incorporated nor registered (see 'Business names' regarding disclosure of ownership). Unlike a company therefore, a partnership has no separate legal identity. For the purposes of legal transaction or litigation, only the members of a partnership can employ people, own property, enter into contracts or be sued. Partnerships, except for professional partnerships such as accountants and solicitors, cannot normally have more than 20 partners. They can, of course, employ people who are not partners. As with sole traders, each partner must tell the Inland Revenue and DSS that they are starting in business.

Management is normally shared amongst the partners but this can be varied by agreement allowing, for example, 'sleeping' partners, who perhaps have contributed some of the capital. It is best at the outset for the partners to draw up a 'Deed of Partnership' with a solicitor. If a deed is not agreed upon then the partnership is governed by the 1890 Act. This will set out the terms and conditions of the partnership; however you should bear in mind that these may be inappropriate to your circumstances.

Profit (income less expenses) is regarded as divided equally between the partners, unless the

Partnership Deed says otherwise. Partners are then assessed for income tax according to their personal circumstances. If a partner does not pay, then other partners can be sued by the Inland Revenue for the money. All partners must pay their National Insurance as for sole traders.

Partnerships have 'unlimited liability', and partners are regarded as being liable both 'jointly and severally'. That is, all partners are regarded as liable for transactions or contracts entered into by any of the partners. The personal assets of a partner may be seized to pay off debts incurred in the course of partnership business. Similarly, all partners may be held responsible for one member's negligence.

It is possible for partnerships to be set up as 'limited partnerships' to protect sleeping partners. A limited partnership (which must register its details with the Registrar of Companies) involves at least one partner who is a 'general partner' – ie has management rights and unlimited liability – and at least one limited partner. A limited partner, who may be an individual or a company, is one who contributes a fixed amount (as capital or property) to the partnership, and who cannot be made liable for partnership debts or liabilities beyond that amount. If you wish to explore this option further you should seek legal advice.

Company

A company is a legal body in its own right, incorporated under the Companies Act 1985, amended in 1989. A small company is usually 'private' – in which case it includes the word 'limited' in its name, (public limited companies include 'plc' in their name). A private company must have at least one shareholder, at least one director and a company secretary (who cannot also be a sole director). The main advantage of trading as a company is limited liability (limited to the initial cost of the shares). However, directors of new companies will almost certainly have to give personal guarantees to banks if seeking loans. A separate legal identity can also be beneficial, for example, allowing the company to continue trading despite the death or resignation of a member.

However, trading as a company brings with it a number of duties and requirements which can add greatly to your administrative and financial load. In order to be incorporated, you must submit the following documents to the Registrar of Companies, with a registration fee (a solicitor can help you to draw these up):

- The Memorandum of Association

- The Articles of Association

- An official declaration of compliance with the requirements of the Companies Act (form G12), and

- A statement of your first directors, secretary and registered office (form G10).

Consideration must also be given to the choice of company name (see below).

Further, companies are required to produce audited accounts and returns and to file an annual report with the Registrar of Companies. Since implementation of the Small Company Audit Exemption Regulations 1994 however, most smaller private limited companies (defined as those with turnover of £90,000 or less and assets not exceeding £1.4 million) are exempt from the audit requirement. Some larger firms can also seek exemption, although if successful they must still provide an accountant's report (called a 'compilation' report).

Both employers and employees, including directors, pay income tax and National Insurance (Class 1) under the Pay As You Earn Scheme. In addition, the company pays 'corporation tax' on any profits.

It is generally advantageous for new businesses to start as sole traders or partnerships; if necessary they can become a company at a later date – it is very difficult to go the other way! One possible reason eventually to become a company is to raise 'equity' finance by issuing shares; there may also be a tax advantage once turnover is high.

Business names

There is no need to register a business unless it is a limited company. Under the Business Names Act 1985 however, the owner and a contact address for any business do have to be disclosed to anyone who may wish to know if:

- The business is known by anything other than the owner's name. So, 'P Brown' does not have to be disclosed, but 'P Brown Repairs' does

- The business is a partnership, in which case the names of all the partners need to be disclosed

- The business is a company which trades under the name other than the company's full name. So 'ABC Textiles (GB) Limited' does not have to be disclosed but 'ABC Textiles' does.

The normal place for disclosure is on all business letters, orders, invoices, receipts and demands for payment of debt. The information must also be displayed prominently at the business premises and all places where you trade.

If a business is carried on under a name other than that of the owner, or owners, the name may require the written approval of the Secretary of State. Certain words cannot be included in a business name, for example, words implying a connection with the Royal Family, government or local authority, or implying national or international pre-eminence. The unauthorised use of certain protected names (often those which refer to a professional status, eg 'architect', 'dentist') may constitute a criminal offence. The Registrar of Companies can advise you of this.

USEFUL TIPS

- *Your business advisor will advise you which form of legal status is most appropriate.*
- *Starting a company costs more, so do not choose this route until you have considered all the advantages and disadvantages. It is possible to buy existing*

or 'ready made' companies, via a Company Registration Agent.

- Always bear in mind your personal circumstances, as each form of business will subject you to different degrees of liability.

16 Business Names Act 1985

This section explains the law on business names and the requirements for disclosure of business ownership.

Introduction

The Companies Act 1981 replaced earlier legislation which required all businesses (not just companies) to register their business name if it was different to those of the proprietors, or if trading under a name different to their corporate name. Businesses are still required to disclose their ownership but the Register of Business Names has been abolished. There is no need to register a business unless it is a limited company, although companies trading under names other than that of the owner or corporation may still need to seek the approval of the Secretary of State. The requirements regarding the use of business names and the disclosure of ownership are set out in the Business Names Act 1985. This legislation has been subject to minor amendments by the Company and Business Names (Amendment) Regulations 1992 and 1995.

Legal restrictions on business names

You will not be allowed to register a company name if:

- It is the same as a name already appearing on the Index of Company names maintained by the Registrar of Companies (Companies House)

- It contains 'limited', 'unlimited' or 'public limited company', or the Welsh equivalents, anywhere in the company name other than at the end

- The Secretary of State considers it offensive or illegal. The use of some words constitutes a criminal offence.

Approval of names

If a business trades under a name other than that of the owner, or owners, or contains certain words, the name may require the written approval of the Secretary of State. Controlled names are set out in statutory regulations. Names which give the impression that the business is connected with Her Majesty's Government (eg 'Crown' or 'Borough') or a local authority might also require permission. A list of such words or expressions can be obtained from Companies House. Sensitive words fall into the following categories:

- Words implying national or international pre-eminence, eg 'International', 'British', 'European'

- Words implying government patronage or sponsorship, eg 'Authority', 'Board', 'Council'

- Words implying business pre-eminence or representative status, eg 'Association', 'Society', 'Institute'

- Words implying specific objects or functions, eg 'Assurance', 'Patent', 'Charter', 'Trust'.

You may also have to obtain the opinion of a relevant national representative body, eg The Architects' Registration Council of the United Kingdom, for a business name including the word 'Architect'. Again, the list may be obtained from Companies House. If you wish to use a word or expression covered in the regulations, you need to submit an application to the Secretary of State at Companies House in either Cardiff (for businesses in England and Wales) or Edinburgh (for businesses in Scotland).

When a business changes hands, the new owner must seek further approval to use a name within 12 months of taking over the business. If a name was registered under the

Registration of Business Names Act 1916 or gained approval under the Companies Act 1981, additional approval is required only when business ownership changes.

Disclosure of ownership

All businesses, whether a sole trader, a partnership or a company, must disclose the name and contact address of the owner, or owners, in writing to anyone wishing to know it. These details must also be shown legibly on all business letters, orders, invoices, receipts and demands for debt. The information must also be displayed at all premises where business is carried out and where you deal with customers and suppliers. There are no requirements on how this information is presented, as long as it is clear and prominent.

You do not need to disclose the owner's name if the business is known by the owner's surname, eg 'W Jones'. If the business is called 'W Jones Bakery', then the owner's name would have to be shown separately.

If the business is a partnership, and the name includes all the partners' names (with or without initials), there is no need to disclose the owners' names again. If there are more than 20 partners then they do not have to be listed on business documents, however, you must supply the address of the principal place of business from which a list of partners can be obtained. You cannot list some of the partners' names and not others, it must be either all or none. If another word is used in the name, then the owners' names must be disclosed separately.

Companies must comply with the disclosure requirements if they trade under a business name different to the full corporate name of the company. Companies must also disclose their registered office address (which may be different from their trading address), their registration number and their place of registration.

A registered company must display its name outside every place of business, in a conspicuous position and in easily legible letters.

Trade marks

If your business or company name has been accepted by the appropriate registry it does not mean it is available for use as a trade mark. By inspecting the index held by the trade mark registry you can determine if there are any prior trade mark rights attaching to your proposed business name.

Exemption from using the word 'limited' in a company name

Certain types of companies can gain exemption from including 'limited' in their company name. These companies must be private companies limited by guarantee. In addition, they must satisfy all of the following conditions:

• The aims of the company must be the promotion of commerce, art, science, education, religion, charity or any profession.

The Memorandum or Articles of Association must state that:

• Any profits or other income are to be spent in promoting the company's objectives

• No dividends are to be paid to members

• If the company is wound up, all the assets are to be transferred to another body which has similar objectives or which promotes charity.

Exemption from using the word 'limited' can be granted after the formation of the company, but this will incur additional costs of £50. Once the exemption is granted, the company will no longer have to comply with the requirements of the Companies Act 1985 relating to the publication of its name and sending lists of members to the registrar. The company is forbidden to alter its articles or memorandum in such a way that it no longer complies with the above conditions.

Failure to comply

Failure to comply with these requirements may result in fines and the loss of certain legal rights. You may lose the ability to enforce contracts which have been entered into under these conditions.

USEFUL TIP

● *The Business Names Act does not cover all of the law relating to the use of business names. There are a number of other Acts dealing with the use of certain words or expressions, and the rights of others over the use of certain names or words. You should consult a solicitor before choosing a particular business name.*

17 Choosing and using a management consultant

This section is a guide to finding a suitable management consultant and to the services they can provide.

Introduction

Running a business requires a wide range of skills, knowledge and experience. Whilst it is preferable to develop skills and experience in-house, sometimes the expertise has to be bought in. Management consultancy is a professional service used by businesses in two main ways: to study or analyse your problems and advise on what you can do about them, or; to implement an idea, solution, new system, etc which you may have developed or may have been suggested to you.

When to use a management consultant

There are certain situations in which a consultant's contribution is particularly applicable:

- Where unusual difficulties are experienced for the first time and an outside expert can explain their true nature and how they have been overcome in other businesses

- When existing staff have neither the time nor the knowledge to cope with a new project

- When you are not entirely clear about the fundamental causes of your firm's problems

- If you feel that an objective review of the company's operations is necessary.

Areas of work

Management consultancy practices include the following areas of work:

- Strategy

- Organisation design and development

- ISO 9000 and quality management

- Manufacturing systems

- Business planning

- Financial management

- Project management

- Information Technology/Information Systems

- Human resource management

- Marketing

- Design and creativity

- Transport management

- European market.

Consultancies may specialise in particular areas or offer a general management support service. The latter offer a comprehensive range of services, but are usually more expensive, although they offer the speed and flexibility associated with a single source consultancy. Look for a consultant with a record of support for the smaller business.

Selection

Identify the problem

If you have not clearly identified what you want the consultant to do, you will have no means to assess the effectiveness of their work. You may run the risk of the consultant creating a need that was not there in the first place. If the business is in difficulties you may be looking for the consultant to identify the problem. In this case it should be clear that this has a limited time span. What to do about the problem can be agreed as a separate contract. You should have the assignment parameters in writing before you approach anyone. This process also helps you identify the skills you are looking for when choosing a consultant. Most importantly, decide beforehand how much you are prepared to budget for the work.

Short-list consultancies

Once the need has been identified, then a list of consultants can be developed. Professional bodies will supply lists. The Institute of Management Consultants can offer advice on appropriate consultants for particular assignments as described. The Management Consultancy Information Service maintains files on consultancy firms and individuals. Reputation is everything in consultancy; talk to other companies that have used the consultants. The local business press may carry features about local consultancies. Ask consultants for referrals from previous clients and a list of those they have worked with. From these lists, select a short-list of promising candidates and write or phone giving a description of the nature of the assignment.

Meet with your short-list

Brief meetings with the remaining candidates are vital in order to assess whether you will be able to establish a working relationship with the person concerned. Each may submit an outline proposal. These should include a quotation for the work, a work plan, expected deliverables and timescales. Look out for operating costs that the consultant may decide to pass on. Is there a mark up? Look for a professional approach. If the consultant is a disorganised person, you can't expect them to organise your business properly either. In project work, good organisation is critical. Look at the personal CV of the consultant who you will be working with. Do they have appropriate qualifications and experience? Are they members of an appropriate professional body? A good consultant should be willing to learn. Look for someone who knows how to ask questions and listen before they advise, rather than someone who has preconceived ideas and imposes off the shelf solutions.

Cost and contract

A written contract (even if this is just in the form of an exchange of letters) is essential to avoid misunderstandings and to focus work and results. Payment to consultants may be in the form of fixed fees, charges for hours worked and expenses, or a commission based upon results. Costs may be reduced if you can reduce the consultant's administrative work load (eg office facilities, staff to assist, printing facilities, use of a company car). You may wish to start with the consultant for a limited paid period before deciding whether the relationship should continue. This should be clearly stated (with dates) in writing.

Good consultancy is not cheap. They are professionals and expect to earn professional salaries. Realistic fees start at around £300 per day. The leading consultancies can charge over £1,000 per day. You should expect the highest standards from the larger firms. It may be possible to obtain support from the DTI for some consultancy work.

Working relations

The services of the consultant should be regarded as integral with the operating of the company. It is expertise bought in, but still working for you. In this regard, the relationship needs to be managed as with any other part of the business. It may be appropriate to involve the consultant in any regular team meetings. The assignment should be seen in the context of the overall strategic development of the business and so should be assessed and managed in the same way ie according to set targets.

In some cases such close involvement is not appropriate, eg a 'politically' sensitive review of the organisational structure. Setting the assignment and reviewing the end result will be particularly important here.

Ensure you liaise with the consultant regularly. On short intensive assignments they may be working closely with you all the time. If they are with you for a fixed period, see them daily. For extended projects, plan in the dates of review meetings. Be prepared to review schedules as the project develops.

Ensure the consultant will be in a position to give you their best attention. Short intensive assignments are best. A consultant with a large caseload of companies may be overstretched and will waste time in travel, adjusting to different problems, etc.

Evaluation

Evaluation will depend upon the effectiveness of your initial planning of the assignment. In particular it will depend upon how concisely you were able to set objectives and targets for the assignment.

Do not be blinded by science. It is the duty of the consultant to be able to communicate their meaning clearly to you. A good consultant should empower the business, not create dependency. If you are consistently out of your depth (eg with technical detail), you may need further training. You may need to employ someone with the necessary expertise on a permanent basis.

The evaluation will frequently be in the form of a report. The results may not be what you expected. Ensure that the necessary ground work has been done for any research conclusions. Ensure that the consultant has abided by the terms of the contract, in particular timescales. Make sure their invoices are correct. You should both have agreed any changes to the agreement in the course of work in writing.

USEFUL TIPS

- *Choose someone you can trust and with whom you can work comfortably.*

- *Try to absorb as much as possible of the consultant's expertise; treat the process as a learning experience.*

- *Be prepared to listen attentively to the consultant's comments and be willing to admit you may have made mistakes. Never employ a consultant to ratify something which you have already decided.*

- *A good consultant will leave you feeling competent to implement recommended policies, and be willing to provide a reasonable amount of low cost part assignment advice.*

18 **Working with your business adviser**

This section looks at how best to work with your business adviser.

Introduction

According to the Institute of Business Advisers (IBA) business counselling is 'the provision of sound and impartial business advice to potential and established businesses, based upon substantial business experience and knowledge of currently related factors, in order that the clients may benefit from that advice in their subsequent actions'.

The number of free business advice services has grown dramatically in recent years, yet many people are still unaware of the wealth of knowledge and experience available to help them set up in business. The variety of organisations which provide free business advice can be confusing. Business Links (in England) are intended to provide a single enquiry point for the various agencies in local areas. Whatever they are called, advisory services depend upon the professionalism and expertise of the individuals working with small businesses.

Sources of free business advice

There are many reasons for seeking the help of a business adviser. You may be considering self employment although you do not have a specific idea in mind. You may have identified a specific opportunity and be fully committed to developing it into a business. You may already be running a small business. The business could be in trouble, or it could be on the verge of rapid growth. You may have identified a particular problem with which you need to deal. You may need help to develop a new product or service.

These factors will affect your choice of agency. Some agencies are geared to helping people to set up a new business and they normally have close links with training, start up grants, workspace, etc. Advice for established small businesses tends to vary much more. In certain areas it may be available free, in others you may have to pay after a certain number of sessions. Some agencies specialise in helping young people.

A number of organisations concentrate upon matching enquirers with a suitable agency. In England a network of Business Links has been established. They act as a 'one stop shop' for all business enquiries in their area. In Scotland, Scottish Business Shops, in Wales Business

Connect and in Northern Ireland the Local Enterprise Development Unit are good first points of contact. For young people Livewire provides an advice matching service for 16-29 year olds throughout the UK.

What can a business adviser provide?

Objectivity

You can become so involved in your own business that sometimes you cannot see the wood for the trees. It is easy to lose your sense of proportion, especially about your own abilities. A new pair of eyes will help you arrive at a more realistic appraisal of your prospects.

Business concepts and methods

If you have no previous experience of management, an adviser can help you use the well tried tools of business analysis to help you take decisions. At the heart of the 'business-like' approach is the business plan, which is a way of analysing the various elements of the business in order to determine the chances of success. You will learn as you go along. An adviser can help you put the theory into practice.

Contacts and local knowledge

Advisers often have useful commercial contacts, through their clients and their fellow advisers. Most advisers have a sound knowledge of the local area, the main business markets and the general state of the economy.

Experience

It is impossible to have direct experience of every type of business, but experience working in business management enables advisers to ask the right questions to get you thinking along the right lines.

Access to resources

Advisers are usually the main route to the various resources available to help small businesses in your area, ie grants and loans, training courses, premises, etc. Often a package of support can be put together with the adviser's help. The adviser also acts as a reference for lenders. Also, advisers often have a range of useful information at hand which you can use.

How should you be treated?

Everyone has their own style. Many advisers provide excellent business advice, but are not particularly good with people. It is important to persevere. Give your relationship with the adviser a chance to develop. In some cases they may be testing out your commitment, and this may make them seem unfriendly at first. Nonetheless, professional advisers are normally trained in how best to handle advice sessions. There are certain general standards which you can expect.

Feeling comfortable

If it is the first time you have presented a business idea to anyone you may be quite apprehensive. The adviser should make an effort to make you feel comfortable through their approach and general attitude. It is important that you approach the relationship as equals. The adviser should also keep your discussions confidential.

A fair hearing

Advisers are normally trained to listen, to ask key questions and to summarise the things that you have been saying so that you know you have been understood. At the end of the session you should feel that you have developed your own thoughts further. You may even feel that you have been totally wrong all along. Even so, you should feel that you have reached this conclusion by yourself. It is a bad sign if you feel that you have not been given a fair hearing, if you have been constantly interrupted, and if the adviser has been doing all the talking.

Guidance not instruction

The adviser should help you to arrive at your own solutions. They cannot and should not take your decisions for you. Just as you would if you were using a consultant, you should always retain a sense of ownership of your enterprise. You are the one taking the risks, the one taking day to day decisions. You are also the one who must live with the consequences of those decisions. The adviser should help you to develop confidence in your own judgement. If you feel undermined, you should probably look for someone else.

Systematic business analysis

Advisers aim to encourage clients to solve the problem systematically and to enable them to deal with similar problems in the future. You should feel encouraged to develop your own ideas. If an idea does not appear to be feasible, the adviser should help you look at alternatives or to carry out some research to reveal any appropriate adjustments to the idea. In the course of sessions, advisers often explain important terms, concepts and methods. They may give further information and refer you to courses. The adviser should avoid jargon and use straightforward language.

Mutually agreed action points

The way the adviser handles sessions will indicate their professionalism. Do they work to an agenda? Do they make notes? Do they agree action points? Do they keep to action points? Above all, do they prepare? Have they read the business plan? Are they fully aware of your case when they meet with you?

What can the adviser expect from you?

Commitment

Running your own business is a big responsibility. The business adviser will be looking for a degree of commitment which makes the prospects of success realistic. You must bring as much (if not more) to the relationship as the adviser does. You must have a genuine enthusiasm for the enterprise, and some pretty clear ideas of how you expect to make it work. The way you prepare for the first meeting is critical. At the outset, you will need to explain your position and the support you feel you need. When seeking professional support it is standard practice to summarise your requirements in a brief. If you do the same before you meet with your adviser, it will help both of you to understand your mutual aims for the relationship.

Preparation and action

The purpose of any advice is to produce action. If the adviser sees no result from your discussions, they will see the sessions as valueless. It is important to keep to agreed action points, or at least to explain why action did not take place. Discussing action and reporting back on the state of the business will be the starting point of each session. Before each meeting, list the points for discussion, and ensure you cover them.

Openness

To help effectively, the adviser must know how much you know. Do not pretend you understand things when you do not. Ask for clarification. Do not pretend things are better than they are. Be completely frank about your problems and circumstances. If your adviser gives constructive criticism, then it is important that you are open to receiving it. If you feel that you cannot cope with a particular task, let your adviser know.

What should you look for?

The adviser you choose will depend upon your particular needs. If you need a mentor, good all round experience, contacts and a good working relationship will be essential. If you need specialist support, qualifications and experience will be the main thing. If you need access to various grants and loans, advisers with limited business experience, but with relevant knowledge, can be very helpful. As in any working relationship, it helps a great deal if you get on at a personal level.

Most advisers should have some previous experience in management positions. Some advisers have run their own business in the past. Having said this, there are many advisers whose main experience lies in giving business advice, and in close involvement with their client's business. Not all business experience is relevant, especially if the person worked for a large enterprise or institution. Many advisers develop a reputation for giving their clients effective support. Do what you can to find out how well regarded the adviser is. If possible, talk to people who have used the agency in question.

Membership of the Institute of Business Advisers shows that the person is an independent professional, who should work to a specified code of conduct. The Institute of Management Consultants accredits consultants who might typically work with larger businesses. Durham University Business School offer a Certificate and a Diploma in Business Counselling – well established and reputable courses. Look for other business and management qualifications, eg Diploma in Management Studies, Master in Business Administration, etc.

- *As in any working relationship, you will experience difficulties. It is very important that you give the relationship with your adviser a chance to work.*

- *Do not hesitate to ask the adviser, in an informal way, about their qualifications and background. The adviser should feel comfortable about disclosing this type of information.*

Appendices

part
four

part
four

19 **Bibliography**

Introduction

Bob Garratt, *The Fish Rots from the Head,* Harper Collins, 1996

Jerry Johnson and Kevan Scholes, *Exploring Corporate Strategy,* third edition, Prentice Hall, 1993

Michael Campbell, Marion Devine and David Young, *A Sense of Mission*, Hutchinson, 1990

John Collins and Gerry Porras, *Built to Last: Successful Habits of Visionary Companies,* Harper Collins, 1994

Gary Hamal and C K Prahalad, *Competing for the Future*, Harvard University Press, 1994

Section 1

Douglas A Gray, *The Entrepreneur's Complete Self-Assessment Guide*, Kogan Page, 1995

Godfrey Golzen, *Working for Yourself*, (sixteenth edition), Kogan Page, 1995

Section 2

Alan West, *A Business Plan*, Pitman, 1991

Bill Richardson, *Business Planning*,
Pitman, 1989

Brian Finch, *Business Plans*,
Kogan Page, 1992

David Irwin, *Financial Control for
Non-financial Managers*, Pitman, 1995

David Irwin, *Planning to Succeed in Business*,
Pitman, 1995

Ron Johnson, *The 24 Hour Business Plan*,
Hutchinson Business Books, 1990

Section 3

Charles Hampden-Turner, *Corporate Culture*,
Hutchinson, 1990

Charles Handy, *Gods of Management*,
Pan, 1995

David Irwin, *Planning to Succeed in Business*,
Pitman, 1995

Gary Hamal and C K Prahalad, *Competing for
the Future*, Harvard University Press, 1994

Michael Campbell, Marion Devine and
David Young, *A Sense of Mission*,
Hutchinson, 1990

Section 4

Gary Jones, *Marketing Decisions*,
Pitman, 1991

Henry Mintzberg, *The Rise and Fall of
Strategic Planning*, Prentice Hall, 1994

Michael Goold and John Quinn,
Strategic Control, Ashridge, 1990

Section 5

Best Practice Benchmarking,
Industrial Newsletters Ltd

Bendell, Kelly and Boulter, *Benchmarking
for Competitive Advantage,* Pitman, 1993

Edmund Gray, Larry Smeltzer,
*Analysing the Competitive Environment
Management, The Competitive Edge,*
Macmillan Publishing Co, 1989

Michael Porter, *Competitive Strategy:
Technique for Analysing Industries and
Competitors,* The Free Press, 1980

Michael Porter, *Competitive Advantage – Creating and Sustaining Superior Performance,* The Free Press, 1985

Section 6

Charles Handy, *Gods of Management,* Pan, 1995

Maureen Bennett, *Managing Growth,* Pitman, 1989

Peter Stannack, *Managing People for the First Time*, Pitman, 1993

Tom Peters and Robert Waterman, *In Search of Excellence,* Harper & Row, 1982

Section 7

Colin Barrow, Robert Brown, Liz Clarke, *The Business Growth Handbook,* Kogan Page, 1995

Jim Brown, *Business Growth Action Kit – A Practical Guide for Expanding Your Business,* Kogan Page, 1995

Maureen Bennett, *Managing Growth,* Pitman, 1989

Section 8

Dale and Plunkett, *Managing Quality*,
Philip Allan, 1990

David Irwin, *Planning to Succeed in Business*,
Pitman, 1995

Dawn Cranswick, *Managing Quality for the First Time*, Pitman, 1996

Quality World, Institute of Quality Management

John S Oakland, *Total Quality Management*,
Butterworth Heinemann Ltd, 1989

Philip B Crosby, *Quality is Free*, McGraw-Hill Book Company, 1979

Philip E Atkinson, *Creating Culture Change: The Key to Successful Total Quality Management*, IFS Publications, 1990

Section 9

Information Management Report,
Elsevier Science

Information Management and Technology,
Cimtech

David A Wilson, *Managing Information*,
Butterworth Heinemann Ltd, 1993

BIBLIOGRAPHY

Section 10

David Irwin, *Planning to Succeed in Business,*
Pitman, 1995

Peter Stannack, *Managing People for the
First Time,* Pitman, 1993

Graham Wilson, *Problem Solving and
Decision Making*, Kogan Page, 1993

Michael Stephens, *Practical Problem Solving
for Managers*, Kogan Page, 1988

Helga Drummond, *Effective Decision Making
A Practical Guide for Management*,
Kogan Page, 1993

Timothy Foster, *101 Ways to Generate Great
Ideas,* Kogan Page, 1991

Section 11

Steven Fink, *Crisis Management,*
Amacorn, 1996

Simon A Booth, *Crisis Management Strategy*,
Routledge, 1993

Section 13

The United Kingdom Franchise Directory,
Franchise Development Services Ltd

Franchise World Magazine, Annual Directory, Franchise World

Martin Mendelsohn, *Guide to Franchising*, Cassell, 1992

Section 14
David Irwin, *Planning to Succeed*, Pitman, 1995

The Big Small Business Guide, Gulliver Books, Evening Standard, 1996

Section 15
Patricia Clayton, *Law for the Small Business*, Kogan Page, 1995

Section 16
Roger Bennett, *Choosing and using a Management Consultant*, Kogan Page, 1990

Directory of Management Consultants in the UK, AP Information Services

20 Useful addresses

Addresses and telephone number for your local **Business Link**, **Training and Enterprise Council (Local Enterprise Company in Scotland)** and **Local Enterprise Agency** may be found in your telephone directory.

The Business Link Signpost service on (0345) 567 765 can put you in touch with your nearest Business Link office. On the Internet at http://www.businesslink.co.uk

Local **Scottish Business Shops** can be contacted on (0141) 248 6014 or (0800) 787 878.

For **Business Connect in Wales** telephone (0345) 969 798.

Local Enterprise Development Unit (LEDU) in Northern Ireland can be contacted on (01232) 491 031.

The National Federation of Enterprise Agencies can put you in touch with your nearest agency. Telephone them on 01234 354055 or on the Internet at http://www.pne.org/cobweb/nfea

Livewire (helps young people to explore the option of starting or developing their own business)
Freepost NT 805
Newcastle upon Tyne, NE1 1BR
Tel: (0191) 261 5584

The Institute of Quality Assurance (IQA)
10 Grosvenor Gardens, London SW1W 0DQ
Tel: (0171) 401 7227

British Quality Foundation
Vigilant House, 120 Wilton Road
London SW1V 1JZ
Tel: (0171) 931 0607

**ASLIB: The Association
for Information Management**
20-24 Old Street
London EC1V 9AP
Tel: (0171) 253 4488

Institute of Management
Management House, Cottingham Road
Corby, Northants NN17 1TT
Tel: (01536) 204 222

British Franchise Association
Franchise Chambers, Thames View
Newtown Road, Henley on Thames
Oxon RG9 1HG
Tel: (01491) 578 049

**National Federation
of Small Businesses**
140 Lower Marsh, Westminster Bridge
London SE1 7AE
Tel: (0171) 928 9272

**The Registrar of Companies
for England and Wales**
Companies House, Crown Way
Cardiff CF4 3UZ
Tel: (01222) 380 801

The London Search Rooms
Companies House, 55-71 City Road
London EC1Y 1BB
Tel: (0171) 253 9393

For Scotland
The Registrar of Companies for Scotland
Companies House, 102 George Street
Edinburgh EH2 3DJ
Tel: (0131) 535 5800

For Northern Ireland
The Registrar of Companies
Department of Commerce, ITB House
64 Chichester Street, Belfast BT1 4JX
Tel: (01232) 234 488

Institute of Management Consultants
5th Floor, 32-33 Hatton Garden
London EC1N 8DL
Tel: (0171) 242 2140

Index

Hawksmere – focused on helping you improve your performance

Hawksmere plc is one of the UK's foremost training organisations. We design and present more than 450 public seminars a year, in the UK and internationally, for professionals and executives in business, industry and the public sector, in addition to a comprehensive programme of specially tailored in-company courses. Every year, well over 15,000 people attend a Hawksmere programme. The companies which use our programmes and the number of courses we successfully repeat reflect our reputation for uncompromising quality.

Our policy is to continually re-examine and develop our programmes, updating and improving them. Our aim is to anticipate the shifting and often complex challenges facing everyone in business and the professions and to provide programmes of high quality, focused on producing practical results – helping you improve your performance.

Our objective for each delegate

At Hawksmere we have one major aim – that every delegate leaves each programme better equipped to put enhanced techniques and expertise to practical use. All our speakers are practitioners who are experts in their own field: as a result, the information and advice on offer at a Hawksmere programme is expert and tried and tested, practical yet up-to-the-minute.

Our programmes span all levels, from introductory skills to sophisticated techniques and the implications of complex legislation. Reflecting their different aims and objectives, they also vary in format from one day multi-speaker conferences to one and two day seminars, three day courses and week long residential workshops.

Our programmes cover a wide variety of subject areas:

- Management development
- Finance
- Marketing and sales
- PR and communications
- Business law
- Acquisitions and disposals
- Commercial agreements
- Entertainment
- Personnel and employment law
- Litigation and ADR
- Insurance and reinsurance
- Commercial and contracts management
- Purchasing and procurement
- Project management and engineering
- Government contracts
- Property and facilities management
- Health and safety
- Information technology management
- British standards in practice

For a brochure on any particular area of interest or for more information generally, please call Hawksmere Customer Services on 0171 824 8257 or fax on 0171 730 4293.

Hawksmere In-company Training

In addition to its public seminars Hawksmere works with client companies developing and delivering a wide range of tailored training in industries as diverse as retailing, pharmaceuticals, public relations, engineering and service industries such as banking and insurance – the list is long.

We offer a unique range of business programs designed to provide middle and senior managers with the tools and techniques to successfully manage their business in today's competitive environment.

Hawksmere trainers are all professionals with sound practical experience. Our approach is participative, with extensive use of case studies and group work. The emphasis is on working with clients to define objectives, develop content and deliver in the appropriate way. This gives our clients total flexibility and control. In our experience, direct client involvement and support are prime contributors to the success of any programme.

Hawksmere In-Company tailored training provides:

- Programmes producing real results
- Expert speakers matched to your company profile
- Flexibility of time and place
- Maximum impact on productivity through training your staff at a pace to suit you

The Hawksmere In-Company team is headed by Aileen Clark, who has worked extensively in management training and development for the past twenty years, building successful courses for a wide range of businesses in both the public and private sectors. Call Aileen or her team on 0171 824 8257 for expert advice on your training needs without any obligation.

Thorogood: the publishing business of the Hawksmere Group

Thorogood publishes a wide range of books, reports, special briefings, psychometric tests and videos.

Listed below is a selection of key titles.

Masters in Management

Mastering business planning and strategy
Paul Elkin   £19.95

Mastering financial management
Stephen Brookson   £19.95

Mastering leadership
Michael Williams £19.95

Mastering negotiations
Eric Evans £19.95

Mastering people management
Mark Thomas £19.95

Mastering project management
Cathy Lake £19.95

The Essential Guides

The essential guide to buying
and selling unquoted businesses
Ian Smith £25

The essential guide to business
planning and raising finance
Naomi Langford-Wood & Brian Salter £25

The essential business guide to the Internet
Naomi Langford-Wood & Brian Salter £19.95

Other titles

The John Adair handbook of management
and leadership – *edited by Neil Thomas*
£19.95

The handbook of management fads
Steve Morris £8.95

The inside track to successful management
Dr Gerald Kushel £16.95

The pension trustee's handbook (2nd edition)
Robin Ellison £25

Reports and Special Briefings

Dynamic budgetary control
David Allen £95

Evaluating and monitoring strategies
David Allen £95

Software licence agreements
Robert Bond £125

Negotiation tactics for software and
hi-tech agreements
Robert Bond £165

Achieving business excellence, quality and
performance improvement
Colin Chapman and Dennis Hopper £95

Legal liabilities for insurers
Fred Collins £95

Effective techniques for managing
and handling insurance claims
Fred Collins £95

Employer's liability and industrial diseases
Fred Collins £95

Compliance with CDM regulations
Stuart Macdougald-Denton £125

Employment law aspects of mergers
and acquisitions – *Michael Ryley* £125

Techniques for successful
management buy-outs – *Ian Smith* £125

Financial techniques for business
acquisitions and disposals – *Ian Smith* £125

Techniques for minimising the risks of
acquisitions: commercial due diligence
Ian Smith & Kevin Jewell £125

Mergers and acquisitions – confronting
the organisation and people issue
Mark Thomas £125

An employer's guide to the management of
complaints of sex and race discrimination
Christopher Walter £125

Securing business funding from
Europe and the UK – *Peter Wilding* £125

Influencing the European Union
Peter Wilding £125

Standard conditions of commercial contract
Peter Wilding £139

To order any title, or to request more information,
please call Thorogood Customer Services on
0171 824 8257 or fax on 0171 730 4293.